METALLICA

THE DEFINITIVE METALLICA!

A VISUAL DOCUMENTARY BY MARK PUTTERFORD & XAVIER RUSSELL

OMNIBUS PRESS
LONDON · NEW YORK · SYDNEY

Edited by Chris Charlesworth
Cover & Book Designed by 4i Limited
Picture research by David Brolan

ISBN: 0.7119.3081.3
Order No. OP 47044

Exclusive Distributors:
Book Sales Limited
8/9 Frith Street,
London W1V 5TZ England

Music Sales Corporation
257 Park Avenue South,
New York, NY 10010 USA

Music Sales Pty. Limited
120 Rothschild Street,
Rosebery, NSW 2018, Australia

To the Music Trade only:
Music Sales Limited
8/9 Frith Street,
London W1V 5TZ England

Photo Credits: Front cover & 1: Ross Halfin
Back cover photographs: LFI/Retna/LFI/Ross Halfin
All Action: 59c, 73; Jay Blakesberg/Retna: 62c&bl, 68b;
Steve Double/Retna: 17c, 19cl, 60b, 64b; Steve
Double/SIN: 2/3, 71; Famous: 16, 19tr, 42t, 79b; Martin
Goodacre/SIN: 76/77; William Hale: 8/9, 12, 13, 15;
Michael Johansson/Retna: 22c, 36t, 68t; Robin
Kaplan/Retna: 31; Todd Kaplan/Starfile: 51, 52t, 76l; Tim
Keenan/SIN: 37, 49b, 50/51, 61tr, 61c; Bob
Leafe/Starfile: 70; London Features International: 6, 7, 9,
10, 11t&b, 17b, 20, 23b, 36b, 38/39, 43b, 48, 55t, 58,
62tr, 72b, 75c, 78; Ross Marino/Retna: 3, 18t&b, 47b;
Mergemeet: 20/21 (x16), 27t&b, 29; Frank
Micelotta/Retna: 22b, 61b, 64t; Gordon Milne: 59c; Tony
Mottram/Retna: 6/7, 18c, 19br, 22, 25, 26, 33, 35, 42b,
43b, 59c, 60c, 63(x2); Katia Natoya/Retna: 71t; Neal
Preston/Retna: 79t; Chuck Pulin/Starfile: 80b; Mike
Putland/Retna: 59r; Relay: 14, 91cr, 24(x5), 44t, 45t&b,
60t, 72t, 80; Retna: 47; Zbysiu Rodak?SIN: 28, 53, 74,
77; Guy Wade/Starfile: 22t; 59c; Justin Thomas/All
Action: 59c, 62tl; Timothy White/Retna: 5, 17t, 19tc,
58b; Kevin Williams: 23c, 41, 49t, 55b, 57, 62br, 65,
66/67(x7), 68c, 75r; Vinnie Zuffante/Starfile: 69.

Printed in the United States of America by
Vicks Lithograph and Printing Corporation

ACKNOWLEDGEMENTS
For their kind assistance in the preparation of this book
the authors would like to express their special thanks to
Gem Howard, Johnny Z, Brian Slagel, Brian Tattler, Sean
Harris, Malcolm Dome, Andy Martin and Ian Jones.

Thrash's maniacal
manifesto was that
it should be the loudest
of the loud, lowest of the
low, 78rpm Metal packed
into 33rpm grooves.

INTRODUCTION

Heavy Metal, the great-grandchild of the blues, the grandson of rock'n'roll and the love child of Sixties psychedelia, has always been the black sheep of rock's family tree. It is anti-social, loud, distorted, dark and dangerous, the antithesis of chart and radio fodder, and always likely to profit from exploitation of generation gaps.

Metal is for a minority. Unperturbed by any need to conform and oblivious of media-courtship or crossover recognition, it moves at its own pace, sometimes hardly at all. It either retreats into its own shadowy circles, derided by the masses and misunderstood by most, or advances like a monster with meat in its mouth, never worrying about popular taste, never wanting to be flavour of the month.

Indeed, whenever Metal has managed to register on the pop charts, it is generally the result of a cynical submission to accessibility which alienates the faithful. But as Metal grew heavier and sank to deeper extremes, its limbs not only stretched to embrace the concept of commerciality, but also reversed into a maze of subdivisions guaranteed to offend commercial instincts.

Thus, after punk's kamikaze mission to destroy the soul of late Seventies rock inertia, Metal bands were left with a disembowelled body to embalm and, with the shock waves from The Sex Pistols still reverberating around the scene, a pretty good idea of how to go about it. The Metal tag was unashamedly snatched up by the younger generation, and a harder, hungrier, harsher descendant of the dynasty was born: a brat some commentators called the New Wave Of British Heavy Metal.

During the early Eighties this itself would subdivide into Black Metal, Death Metal, Doom Metal, Thrash Metal, Speed Metal, Power Metal, Punk Metal, Hate Metal, Grindcore and any number of other grotesque variations on the theme, but in its purest form the NWOBHM (as its more intimate associates would have it) was simply a fresher slant on established values of banshee vocals, garrotting guitars and jack-hammer drums. As rock in its broadest form underwent some kind of renaissance in the UK during the first two years of the new decade, so the cream of the NWOBHM sunk their talons into the heels of the more established artists who were enjoying the novelty of (albeit moderate) chart success, and dragged themselves into the rarified realm of radio play.

In 1981 - the very year James Hetfield met Lars Ulrich and discussed the possibility of doing some Metalwork of their own - Metal of the particularly Heavy

charts in an orderly fashion. The Deep Purple fragmentations of Rainbow, Gillan and Whitesnake competed for popular preference, while the likes of Thin Lizzy, UFO, Judas Priest and Rush also made brief acquaintances with the Top 20. Of the NWOBHM bands only Saxon, Iron Maiden and Girlschool managed similar achievements with Def Leppard not far behind, but none of the aforementioned hit the jackpot at the very summit of the charts - a cosy corner roped off for the likes of Abba, Cliff Richard, Adam And The Ants, Phil Collins and Stars On 45 - and most had to forego their more intense inclinations to even make the grade at all.

Except Motörhead. When the live 'No Sleep Til Hammersmith' album crashed straight into the UK charts at number one on June 27, 1981, it represented one of the most influential Metal bands of the era at the peak of their popularity, unwittingly providing a source of inspiration for scores of school-leaving scum-bags who scorned

MOTÖRHEAD: LEMMY, PHILTHY AND 'FAST' EDDIE CLARKE.

kind was a stranger to the upper echelons of either singles or album charts. In America, where there's hardly ever been a pop scene as such and 'rock' is the term designed to cover a multitude of dins, the only rock bands to intrude in the Top 20 were those who'd coated themselves with the necessary layers of melodic sugar: Journey, REO Speedwagon, Styx, Loverboy, Pat Benatar, Heart... you know the form. Even Van Halen had toned their act down by this time, while perhaps the heaviest of all the rock bands in the US charts during 1981, AC/DC, notched up one of the best-selling Metal albums of all time ('Back In Black') by laying themselves at the mercy of a producer (Mutt Lange) who clearly had FM waves where others have only ear wax.

In Britain, 1981 saw a glut of renowned remnants of the Seventies file into the

the very notion of compromise in their quest for megawatt nirvana. Not least Messrs Hetfield and Ulrich over in LA, who would soon be moulding their typical teenage angst and aggression around something very similar.

Indeed, how ironic that exactly a decade on in the summer of 1991 an horrendously heavy album called 'Metallica' should crash into charts all around the world at number one - a remarkable achievement, particularly in America where the top spot is the traditional sanctuary of mind-numbing MOR - and that a band of the same name should achieve the acclaim of being as influential as those who influenced them, hauling Metal from the fringes of supersonic insanity to the mainstream chartland itself. It has been an unprecedented crossover of breathtaking magnitude.

BRUCE DICKINSON WITH SAMSON
DURING THE HEIGHT OF THE NWOBHM.

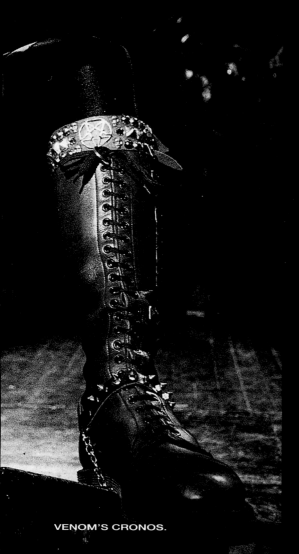

VENOM'S CRONOS.

not least with fellow countrymen like Slayer, Anthrax, Exodus and Megadeth, and Europeans like Kreator, Helloween, Celtic Frost and Destruction. But in pushing to the front they stuck to their guns and let strange quirks of fate do the rest. It is certainly difficult to imagine anything further from the band's mind than the international pop charts when they kick-started the bandwagon in 1981, but after the excess of success in 1991, it's difficult to imagine them keeping out of the charts for the rest of the millennium.

Of course many of the band's original fans never wanted to see them rubbing shoulders with the likes of Def Leppard, Dire Straits and Madonna - like, that wasn't part of the deal, the exclusivity of the brotherhood would be ruined. This was supposed to be about sweaty little clubs, beaten-up vans, gallons of cheap beer, greasy hair, middle-fingers and a skull-splitting wall of sound that even your older brother would hate. This was not supposed to be about heaving stadia, stretch limos, private jets, posh hotels, champagne and *Top Of The Bleeding Pops*. The band received letters from their fans as long ago as 1984 urging them not to become successful because it would take all the fun out of liking them, and today many dyed-in-the-denim early Eighties fans cannot accept the maturing of Metallica's previous hyperfuzz apocalypse and the consequential broadening of their appeal.

But even if Metallica have 'gone soft', 'wimped out' or 'sold out', they still remain the heaviest, ugliest, most Metallic shower ever to pitch their brutish standard at the summit of the charts. Hetfield, Ulrich, Kirk Hammett and Jason Newsted have achieved far more in transcending the blinkered Thrash genre and notching up multi-platinum returns in 1991 than other in-vogue rogues like Guns n'Roses, with their made-for-radio bad-boy tunes, or Nirvana, on the crest of the Seattle-sound wave.

So cast your mangled minds back to the genesis of it all, focus in on the most significant events of zero hour, 1981: in London Prince Charles marries his Lady Diana, in Washington Ronald Reagan becomes the President of the USA, in Rome The Pope is shot, at Wembley Ricky Villa scores a glorious winner as Tottenham beat Manchester City 3-2 to win the 100th FA Cup Final, and in a Los Angeles suburb called Norwalk two teenage tearaways decide to start a band…

But then that's the essence of the Metallica story: acne-ridden kids trying to emulate their idols, thrashing out a noise that aligns them with an underground movement tired of the corporate norm, and an incredible escalation of street-level popularity which, to complete the cycle, turns the brats of 1981 into the aristocrats of 1991. True, they have compromised along the way, streamlining their bloodbath sound with the inestimable benefits of maturity and experience, but the band that now stands as one of Metal's favourite sons has altered what is recognised as the acceptable face of Metal in a way few but the most perceptive of hardcore connoisseurs could've thought possible at the dawn of the great Thrash Age.

After all, the very bottom line in Thrash's maniacal manifesto was that it should be the loudest of the loud, lowest of the low, 78rpm Metal packed into 33rpm grooves. As New Wave movers like Diamond Head, Samson, Praying Mantis, White Spirit, Angel Witch and Tygers Of Pan Tang nudged the hulking Metallic beast along, a more depraved form yet was skulking in the background: Venom, who headed the Thrash revolution, turning even Motörhead upside down and inside out to produce a wickedly contorted bastard that most NWOBHMers couldn't even grasp, let alone the sanitised souls of radio rock.

And so it was that Metallica took up the challenge from the likes of Venom to regurgitate something even faster, even heavier, even more intense. They jostled for pole position in a hundred-strong field,

Hey, if I put a band together and do an original song will you give us a spot on the album?

Lars Ulrich talking to Brian Slagel

CHAPTER ONE

GARAGE DAYS

JAMES HETFIELD AND RON MCGOVNEY
ON STAGE AT THE OLD WALDORF
THEATER IN SAN FRANCISCO,
OCTOBER 1982.

"Los Angeles in the early '80s was really out of step with what was happening in the wider world of Metal, particularly this amazing scene that was growing in the UK called The New Wave Of British Heavy Metal. Actually I only knew one guy who was into the NWOBHM like I was, a friend of mine called John Kornarens, and we'd go to all the Metal shows around LA together and look out for new bands and stuff. At one show, a Michael Schenker concert at the Country Club around the spring of '81, we saw this kid with a Saxon UK Tour T-shirt on, so John got talking to him about the NWOBHM scene and we ended up getting real friendly and hanging out together. His name was Lars Ulrich.

"Later in the year I started to notice a new Metal scene growing in LA too - bands like Mötley Crüe, Ratt, Black'N'Blue, Malice, Rough Cutt and Armored Saint were happening - so I thought it would be a good idea to do a compilation album with all these bands so people from outside of LA would get to hear them too. When he heard about my idea Lars, who was jamming around with some friends in his garage at the time, called me up and said, 'Hey, if I put a band together and do an original song will you give us a spot on the album?', and I said, 'Absolutely'. That was how Metallica got started."

Brian Slagel, prime mover behind the 'Metal Massacre' compilation albums and boss of LA's Metal Blade Records, recalls the conception of Metallica with a justifiable sense of pride. But the real roots of the band who in turn have helped to make him famous sink way beyond the cavalier opportunism of the 'Hit The Lights' demo which first got the name Metallica (albeit misspelt Mettallica!) into print.

Denmark is probably the most unlikely birthplace of a modern musical phenomenon, probably more so than a

Away from the school courts Lars had found a more alluring use for his racket - as a guitar substitute, to be paraded in front of the bedroom mirror to the strains of Deep Purple.

The young Ulrich was a fanatical Metalhead.

decent pint of lager come to think of it, but that's where the story really starts. Lars Ulrich (aka Large Oilrig), a hyper-talkative, hyperactive kid from a wealthy Copenhagen family, had circled the globe as a young kid watching his father Torben compete in professional tennis tournaments and had even begun to show some talent as a tennis player himself - actually representing his country as a junior and "floating around between number 10 and 15 in my age bracket" in the country. But the truth of the matter was that away from the school courts Lars had found a more alluring use for his racket - as a guitar substitute, to be paraded in front of the bedroom mirror to the strains of Deep Purple.

The young Ulrich was a fanatical Metalhead, and had been since his father, himself a big rock music fan, and a few of his hippy friends took him to a Deep Purple concert in Denmark during February 1973. As a nine-year-old he didn't really understand what was going on, but he was fascinated by the way guitarist Ritchie Blackmore threw his guitar around and made it all look terribly exciting. A week later he started his very own record collection with Purple's 'Fireball' album and, in his own words, "It's all been downhill from there...".

Somewhere along that 'downhill' slope Lars collided heavily with the NWOBHM, and the deflection changed the whole direction of his life. It was around the autumn of 1979 and he'd just returned home from attending a renowned tennis academy in Florida, when a local Heavy Metal record store owner called Ken

Anthony, a leading light on the Danish HM scene who the pop-eyed punter idolised, introduced him to an album called 'Survivors' by the British band Samson. Lars didn't know it at the time but the New Wave was about to engulf him completely.

A few months later, in March 1980, while on another tennis trip to America, he came across Iron Maiden. "I walked into a record store searching for the latest Triumph album or some such shit, and I was over at the import bin poking around. Now, this was still before I was truly aware of what was going on in England, so when I came across an album called 'Iron Maiden' I had no idea who or what they were. The front cover illustration of 'Eddie' could have been done by any one of 100 bands, but the exciting live shots on the back of the sleeve really stood out. There

DEEP PURPLE IN 1973, LEFT TO RIGHT: JON LORD, GLENN HUGHES, DAVID COVERDALE, IAN PAICE AND RICHIE BLACKMORE.

was something so heavy about the whole vibe. What really hooked me was a small shot of the two guitarists, Dave Murray and Dennis Stratton, in the bottom left-hand corner. I'd never seen any band look like this before. Such aggression!"

He bought the album but couldn't play it until he returned home to Denmark in the April because he didn't have access to a record player in America. By then Ken Anthony had uncovered another gem for him to savour - Saxon's 'Wheels Of Steel'

album, "which utterly and completely knocked me out" - and from there on the two of them were on a voyage of discovery.

"The highlight of the week was being invited over to Ken's place to hear all the latest singles that he'd picked up on his regular trips to England. I'd spend hours just looking through all the new releases."

During the September of 1980, with their son's prospective tennis career in mind, the Ulrich family moved permanently to America, settling in the Huntington Beach district south of Los Angeles in Orange County. Though he was removed from the vicinity of the New Wave Metal scene, 16-year-old Lars managed to stay in touch with all the latest noise from Europe.

"I was truly obsessed by the NWOBHM," he confessed to *RAW* magazine. "You see, I landed in the States and there was Van Halen, Journey and Styx happening. None of these new bands had got a look in. America had just about heard of Judas Priest and UFO, who were old warhorses as far as the UK was concerned.

"I kept in touch via *Sounds*, which back then was my Bible. Each week I'd eagerly pore over every printed word in the paper, spending hours going through the whole thing. I had a long list of every single band in the NWOBHM who got a namecheck - even if it was only in the gig guide. I ended up with over 200 names, not knowing that about 180 or so were just garage bands who'd only written one song themselves!"

Lars would also retain regular contact with his old friend Ken Anthony, who'd occasionally send his ex-pat protégé tapes

DIAMOND HEAD.

of New Wave stuff he'd picked up from the edge of obscurity. The names of those bands which then squeezed their way into Ulrich's vast collection now read like a roll-call of fallen soldiers, lost somewhere on the battleground of early eighties rock: Angel Witch, Blitzkrieg, Jaguar, Holocaust, Raven, Sledgehammer, Praying Mantis, White Spirit, Vardis, Tank, Witchfinder General, Savage, Sweet Savage, Witchfynde, Trespass, Gaskin, Hollow Ground, Xero, Paralex... the list tails off into the murky depths of the memory.

But one name maintains an enormous significance even today, a band who looked set to become the biggest NWOBHM noise of them all before Old Father Fate cruelly kicked them in the quavers: Diamond Head.

"The first time I heard Diamond Head was via the 'Helpless'/'Shoot Out The Lights' single," says Lars. "Ken recorded it for me in the summer of 1980. It was good but not outstanding. Then, in one of the September issues of Sounds, I recall seeing a letter from someone who said they'd gotten a copy of the band's mail-order only 'Lightning To The Nations' LP and wanted a track listing for it. That's how I became aware of the fact that Diamond Head did have a bit of a vibe.

"So anyway I sent away for this LP, never got it and sent away again. It took me six to eight months to get the record, but in the meantime I'd struck up a writing relationship with Linda Harris, (lead singer) Sean's mum and co-manager of the band. She wrote really nice letters to me, sent me embroidered patches and singles - but still no album! Finally, in April 1981, the white label arrived and the riffing and the freshness just amazed me.

"I also recall a compilation album, 'Brute Force', which featured a track from Diamond Head titled 'It's Electric' that was unbelievable! And if you take a look at the sleeve of the record now and compare

the photo of Diamond Head with all the other groups there, they had an attitude and a vibe about them that none of the others could match. There was something special about Diamond Head - no doubt about it!"

Such was Lars' obsession with the Stourbridge-based quartet he even flew over to England during the summer of 1981 to catch the band's UK tour. Turning up on the last night of the tour at Woolwich Odeon in London on July 10, he charmed his way backstage and clung on to the coat-tails of the band so tightly that he ended up getting a lift back to the Midlands in their camper van and the offer of spending the night at Sean Harris' house.

"He ended up staying a week," Sean laughs in recollection. "We couldn't get rid of him! But it was a bit of a novelty for us because he was the first foreigner to get into the band, so we didn't mind his attentions because we thought we must be doing something right if a kid is going to fly all the way from California to see us.

"Lars was a really nice kid too, and such a big fan it was frightening. He'd stay up all night listening to 'It's Electric'. I'd sit up with him until the early hours, fall asleep, wake up a few hours later, and he'd still have the damn record on!"

After staying at Sean's for a week he then spent a week sleeping on guitarist Brian Tatler's bedroom floor in a dirty old sleeping bag, hanging out with the band and even getting the chance to see them live again at Hereford, a show for which 18 people turned up if Sean's memory serves him correctly. The two of them went to see the 'Heavy Metal Holocaust' concert (featuring Motörhead, Blizzard Of Ozz, Triumph, Mahogany Rush and Riot) at Port Vale football ground in August, and built up a friendship which remains strong to this day.

"Lars just wanted to know everything about Diamond Head," says Brian. "He was really wide-eyed about it all. He'd stay up

all night at our house watching rock videos - his favourite clip of all was the guitar solo sequence in 'Freebird' from when Lynyrd Skynyrd did Knebworth in 1976, he'd go mad to that.

"One thing that amazed me about Lars was the way he would spend money on records and stuff. He'd have hundreds of pounds on him, even though he was just a

> "The funny thing was, he never mentioned anything about starting a band at that time, and I'm not even sure he could play the drums then. But he never once mentioned Metallica..."

kid, and he'd go into record shops and buy piles and piles of NWOBHM stuff. He was even going to buy all my old copies of Sounds off me at one point.

"The funny thing was," Brian adds, "he never mentioned anything about starting a band at that time, and I'm not even sure he could play the drums then. I mean, he'd watch us soundchecking at gigs and stuff, and I feel sure that if he could've played then he would've asked us for a bash, because that's the kind of forward-type kid he was. He used to talk about playing tennis all the time, and he never stopped talking about all the bands he liked, but he never once mentioned Metallica..."

Back home in the States, inspired by his friendship with Brian and Sean and also Lemmy from Motörhead, whose hotel room floor he'd decorated with the aftermath of an ill-advised vodka drinking session, Lars decided to try to put his own band together. He did actually fancy himself as a drummer although he was too

SEAN HARRIS FROM DIAMOND HEAD, ADOPTING ROBERT PLANT POSE.

JAMES HETFIELD IN 1982.

garage whenever they were out, and James would sneak in and tinker around on the keyboards with an increasing degree of fascination.

Hetfield actually took two painful years of piano lessons while at grade school before turning with some relief ("I wanted to make noise, not study theory") to the guitar at junior high. His mother bought him "a $15 job" electric guitar and he painted it to look like those of his idols', initially like the Gibson SG used by Tony Iommi from Black Sabbath and then like one of Eddie Van Halen's striped models. However, it wasn't until his brother took him to Long Beach Arena in 1978 to see Aerosmith and AC/DC that James experienced his first rock concert, and that's when the band bug bit him hardest; he wanted to be up there on that stage himself, in front of all those people, making all that noise.

Hetfield's first bands were high school outfits that went under names like Leather Charm and Obsession, the latter a cover group which would gig around the local halls the way high school cover groups do. From time to time James would try to get the others to play some of the songs he'd written himself, but they felt they'd get

The most interesting reply he got was from an 18-year-old high school graduate and Black Sabbath fan called James Hetfield, who worked in a print shop but claimed he could play guitar and sing a bit as well.

embarrassed to admit it to the Diamond Head chaps. Even as a child he would hit cardboard boxes with paint-stirrers and pretend to be Deep Purple's Ian Paice, and in 1976, aged 12, he'd wangled a modest kit out of his grandmother by sinking to his knees, assuming a humble praying pose and "saying 'please, please, please' about fifty thousand times". But until now he'd fought shy of actually forming a proper band.

His first move was taking the time-honoured step of placing an ad in a local LA newspaper, and the most interesting reply he got was from an 18-year-old high school graduate and Black Sabbath fan called James Hetfield, who worked in a print shop but claimed he could play guitar and sing a bit as well, despite being known for his taste for Venom merchandise. Hetfield was actually a native of suburban Los Angeles who, like Lars, had been flirting with music from an early age. His elder brother Dave played drums in a band called The Bitter End which would rehearse in James' parents'

better reactions from their crowds if they stuck to songs everyone knew, and hence the seeds of Hetfield's discontent in the cover scene were sown. While he wanted to get serious about it and move on to the next stage, his friends just wanted to play safe. That's when he came across the ad placed by Lars.

Hetfield had in fact been pestered by Ulrich to form a band before, but after rehearsing with him and a friend called Hugh Tanner he'd decided that this hyper little Dane couldn't play drums to save his life. "I admit it, I was absolute fucking crap back then," Lars was to admit years later, adding that his kit was so flimsy the cymbals used to fly through the room every time he hit them. But such honesty didn't help matters at the time, and Hetfield sensibly knocked the whole idea on the head.

The next time Lars contacted James, however, he was able to dangle the carrot of the 'Metal Massacre' album before him, and this was clearly an offer he couldn't turn down. With some reservations about working with Ulrich he nevertheless agreed to give the demo a shot, handling bass and vocals and roping in another local kid, a black guitarist called Lloyd Grant, to complete the line-up. It was hardly the joining together of great musical forces, more a marriage made in hell that was destined for a quickie divorce, but as far as the very bottom rung of the ladder went, it was about the best they could muster for now.

"When I told him I'd give him the chance to be on the 'Metal Massacre I' album, Lars called me and said, 'Look, we're gonna have to do this on a four-track recorder, is that OK?', Brian Slagel recalls. "They were just kids playing around in a garage and didn't have the money or probably the ability to produce a first-class recording. Now at the time I didn't have much money either, so I just told him, 'Sure man, just do the best you can'."

On their tiny four-track TEAC machine they came up with 'Hit The Lights', a title not unlike Diamond Head's 'Shoot Out The Lights'. They persuaded another local kid called Dave Mustaine, who got the job after ten days' rehearsing with a surfer simply remembered as Mike failed to impress James and Lars, to overdub some lead guitar. It was very garagey, rougher than a sandpaper condom, but it stated clearly enough where the band were at and managed to leave some impression on those who got to hear it.

"A few of us would mock Lars when he said he was going to start a band," says Slagel, "because it just didn't seem possible that our friend could be up there doing that sort of thing. He'd be saying, 'Oh yeah, I'm gonna be headlining all the bars around here soon', and we'd say, 'Oh sure Lars, of course you are'. So when we got to hear 'Hit The Lights' we started to think, 'Hmmm, maybe something is going to come out of all of this...'"

No one could've guessed the size of

They persuaded another local kid called Dave Mustaine, who got the job after ten days' rehearsing with a surfer simply remembered as Mike failed to impress James and Lars, to overdub some lead guitar

It was very garagey, rougher than a sandpaper condom.

THE BIBLE OF HEAVY METAL

Encyclopedia Metallica

Compiled by Brian Harrigan and Malcolm Dome.

...ull story of Heavy Metal from Cream and Jimi Hendrix ...ugh Led Zeppelin to today's top bands, Def Leppard, ...n Maiden and AC/DC. Packed with action photos, ...iographical details and recommended listening.

the giant oak which would grow from such a tiny acorn, least of all Brian Slagel who originally pressed only 4,500 copies of the 'Metal Massacre' compilation album (which also featured Steeler, Bitch, Malice, Ratt, Avatar, Cirith Ungol, Demon Flight and Pandemonium) for his newly formed label, Metal Blade. Slagel even made the mistake of licensing the record to another US company called Metalworks, who had bid for it on the basis that they were going to get major backing and make everyone a fortune out of it, but in the event certain promises weren't kept and Metal Blade finally won the rights to the record back some years later. However, after shifting another 10,000-plus copies Metal Blade once again became embroiled in a legal battle, this time with their distributors Enigma, and the record is currently out of print once more.

Metallica and Metal Blade just never seemed destined for each other, their professional relationship apparently jinxed from the moment their name was spelt wrongly on the artwork for 'Metal Massacre'. Ulrich and Hetfield toyed with Red Vette and Blitzer before settling on Metallica, but when they finally submitted the name to Metal Blade and the sleeve artist misspelt it with an extra 't', finances were so low that Slagel couldn't afford to have the graphics re-designed correctly. By the same token, Ron McGovney became Ron McGouney and Lloyd Grant became Llyod Grant!

"I just had to shrug my shoulders, apologise to the guys, and put it out as it was," he laughs. "By that time I'd spent my $2,000, or whatever it was I had set aside for the album, and so that was it. Of course I never thought it was that important then..."

Although the expression 'Metallica' was first used in the title of an HM reference book - *Encyclopedia Metallica* - published by Omnibus Press in 1981 and written by UK journalists Brian Harrigan and Malcolm Dome, the name was actually stolen from an Oregon-based fanzine run by two friends of Lars', fanatical Metal fans called Ron Quintana and Ian Kallen. Quintana had told Ulrich about his plans for a fanzine called *'Metallica'* - who knows, maybe he

DAVE MUSTAINE BACKSTAGE AT THE WALDORF, 1982.

originally got the idea from *Encyclopedia Metallica*? - whereupon the drummer suggested that *'Metal Mania'* was a far better name for a fanzine... and promptly bagged the name for himself!

Lloyd Grant soon left the fold and by the time 'Metal Massacre I' had caused a bit of a buzz on the underground Metal scene in America, the line up of the band calling itself Metallica was Hetfield on vocals, Mustaine on guitar, Hetfield's roommate Ron McGovney on bass and Ulrich on drums. The four would rehearse a mixture of original material and cover tunes at the Ulrich domain in Huntington Beach, eventually managing to demo (Savage's) 'Let It Loose' and (Sweet Savage's) 'Killing Time' to add to their initial recording of 'Hit The Lights'. Indeed, it was on the strength of that demo that Metallica were offered their first notable gig, supporting Saxon at the Whiskey A-Go-Go on Sunset Boulevard in West Hollywood, March 5, 1982.

"Saxon were playing four shows at the Whiskey - two sets a night, two nights running," Brian Slagel remembers, "and it was quite a gig for Metallica to land, especially as Saxon were one of the biggest NWOBHM bands at that time. To be honest, Metallica weren't very good if I remember rightly, but it was a start."

From there the band picked up gigs wherever they could in LA - The Troubadour, The Roxy, The Country Club, The Starwood, any local dive that'd put them on - and built their set around a number of NWOBHM covers (Diamond Head's 'The Prince', 'Am I Evil', 'Helpless' and 'Sucking My Love', Savage's 'Buried Alive' and 'Let It Loose', Sweet Savage's 'Killing Time' and 'Blitzkrieg' by Blitzkrieg), none of which would actually be introduced to the audience as covers in the hope that the fans would think they were all Metallica originals.

At one infamous LA gig the band were called on to open for Swiss outfit Krokus, but had to play the show on their own after the headliners pulled out at the last minute. Such was the impact of this performance, so the band like to claim, that the event became known as The Night Of Metallica.

Their first proper strides recording-wise came shortly after this when, on the obligatory shoestring budget, they scraped together a demo tape of seven original songs, a package they titled

"The LA audiences thought Metallica were a punk band... although even the punk bands weren't as fast as this.

'No Life Til Leather' (with an obvious nod towards Motörhead's 'No Sleep Til Hammersmith'). It was the classic garage band tape - ridiculously rough and with scant regard for the art of mixing (the bass, for starters, was far too loud). But those underground fiends who heard it agreed there was something

different brewing beneath the white-noise façade, and the seeds of a buzz were sown.

The tracks were 'Hit The Lights' (short, sharp and very fast, a natural show-opener); 'The Mechanix' (very much a Mustaine favourite, so much so that when he later quit Metallica to form Megadeth he revamped

The Metal scene in San Francisco was far healthier for bands of the 100mph persuasion during 1982. A network of underground fans - known affectionately as the Bay Area 'Bangers - had precipitated the emergence of fanzines like *Metal Mania*.

the track for their 'Killing Is My Business... And Business Is Good' album); 'Motorbreath' (a double reference to Motörhead and the motormouth inclinations of Ulrich, but not one of the band's best efforts); 'Seek And Destroy' (a future Metalliclassic, sometimes referred to as 'She Can Destroy'); 'Metal Militia' (one of the band's fastest ever tracks, and a milestone in the Thrash movement of the early 1980s); 'Jump In The Fire' (a slower song, strangely omitted from some copies of 'No Life...'); 'Phantom Lord' (incredibly heavy with a constantly changing tempo, crammed full of squealing guitar solos).

Although quite rare these days, the 'No Life Til Leather' demo is still considered by some to represent the birth of Thrash Metal itself. Other observers - including Lars Ulrich - insist that honour should be bestowed on Newcastle's Venom, whose début album 'Welcome To Hell' was released in 1981. Nevertheless, for the glammmy Los Angeles of 1982, Metallica's white-hot desire to be faster, harder, louder and more overwhelmingly intense than anything else on the face of the planet was a novelty that could hardly be ignored.

"The LA audiences thought Metallica were a punk band," says Brian Slagel, "although even the punk bands weren't as fast as this. The problem was that at this time the glam scene had taken over in LA with bands like Mötley Crüe and Ratt starting to come through, so nobody really knew what to do with Metallica. In the end we decided to take the band further afield, and so we put together a 'Metal Massacre' package of Bitch, Metallica and Cirith Ungol, which we planned to take to San Francisco. Unfortunately, Cirith Ungol didn't make it, but the shows we did at The Stone in Frisco with Metallica were amazing, and the response the band got was totally overwhelming."

The Metal scene in San Francisco was far healthier for bands of the 100mph persuasion during 1982. A network of underground fans - known affectionately as the Bay Area 'Bangers - had precipitated the emergence of fanzines like *Metal Mania* and a number of record stores which thrived on import sales and revelled in the obscurity of their stock. Perhaps the most popular of these was the Record Vault on Polk Street, which offered the local fanatics a selection of

himself amid something akin to the great 1906 earthquake. In the mayhem, he dropped his five-pint pitcher of beer.

The main feature of Metallica's 'Metal Monday' shows was the sheer speed with which they played heavyweight works like 'The Mechanix', 'Phantom Lord', 'Jump In The Fire', 'No Remorse' and 'Metal Militia'. This was later described as 'Motörhead on speed' or a sort of 'Heavy Metal Ramones', but whatever analogies the early reporters grasped at, everyone agreed they hadn't seen anything quite like it.

At its heart the maelstrom was fuelled by a vicious, seething ego-battle between Mustaine and Hetfield. Mustaine, fuelled by various intoxicating substances, roared to the forefront as lead guitarist, demanding centre stage like a man possessed. Hetfield, now playing rhythm guitar and refusing to be shoved aside, fought back with crazy antics of his own, desperately matching Mustaine's every move. The electricity created between the two simply intensified the general abandon of the performance, although on occasions it spilled over from sheer enthusiasm into nasty scenes of rivalry.

Back in Los Angeles at the end of the year, however, Ulrich and Hetfield - the self-appointed nucleus of the group - decided that if the band was going to progress towards a more professional league a few changes would have to be made. For a start, problems had arisen with Dave Mustaine which went beyond simple onstage competition.

"Dave was an incredibly talented guy," says Brian Slagel, "but he also had an incredibly large problem with alcohol and drugs. He'd get wasted and become a real crazy person, a raging maniac, and the other guys just couldn't deal with that after a while. I mean, they all drank of course, but I guess they could all hold their liquor better than Dave, and I could see they were beginning to get fed up of seeing Dave drunk out of his mind all the time."

skull-splitting bric-a-brac such as back issues of *Kerrang!*, old bootlegs and new demos from local groups such as Exodus, Trauma, Vicious Rumors, Overdrive, Laaz Rockit, Heathen and Anvil Chorus.

All the bands would hang out at the Record Vault, along with the import-mad Ulrich and other colourful characters on the scene. One of these, a self-proclaimed Bay Area 'Bangeress by the name of Kathi Page, worked for the local radio station KRQR, one of the few rock stations that didn't exist on a staple diet of Journey, Jefferson Starship and Styx, and she quickly realised the need for all these bands to have a regular live outlet.

By October 1982 Page had persuaded KRQR to sponsor and promote a weekly rock night at the Old Waldorf club in the city's downtown financial district. Conveniently titled 'Metal Monday', it presented three new Metal acts at the beginning of each week, usually from the Bay Area of the city, and despite competition from the regular Monday night dose of live football from the NFL, the event's popularity swiftly translated into healthy attendance figures.

Undoubtedly the most popular of all the bands featured at Metal Mondays were Metallica, who started off occupying the middle-slot on the bill. Before long the Bay Area Bangers adopted the band as their own and gave them the kind of reception which more often than not intimidated the headliners. On one occasion co-author Russell caught a Laaz Rockit/Metallica/Overdrive show and found

At its heart the maelstrom was fuelled by a vicious, seething ego-battle between Mustaine and Hetfield. Mustaine, fuelled by various intoxicating substances, roared to the forefront as lead guitarist, demanding centre stage like a man possessed.

CLIFF BURTON AND LARS, 1983.

decided that bassist Ron
sn't really pulling his weight
er. He often seemed to be
nstage, giving the
Slagel at least that "he
edicated to the cause". To
riction, Hetfield had voiced
ort with his role as lead
gested he reverted to
st, handing over vocal duties
e Armored Saint's John

had a much clearer vision of the path
Metallica should take the moment they
crossed paths with a bass player by the
name of Cliff Burton. With McGovney out of
the picture Hetfield, Ulrich and Mustaine,
given another chance to get his act
together, had started searching for a
replacement when they were alerted by
reports of a madcap player from a San
Francisco outfit called Trauma, who
ironically featured on Metal Blade's

persuade Burton to change his mind, the
band surrendered and agreed to relocate
themselves to San Francisco, where they
seemed more eagerly welcomed by Meta
fans than in LA anyway. At their first
rehearsal together, at friend/roadie Mark
Whittaker's house, they set up their gear
and by the end of the first song, 'Seek An
Destroy', everyone agreed Burton was th
man for the job.

Burton duly quit Trauma and began

TOP LEFT: THE ORIGINAL HAND-WRITTEN
LYRICS TO THE SONG "BLITZKRIEG";
INSET: METALLICA'S ORIGINAL
CALLING CARD, CIRCA 1982.

INSET: METALLICA'S PHARMACY SET.
NOTE ABSENCE OF "ABSOLUT VODKA"

LICA

DAMAGE INC.

1986

Yo, THE ROYAL DANISH FAMILY
SEND THEIR LOVE! WELL
SO GUESS WHAT! THINGS
ARE REALLY FLYING HERE
IN THE STUDIO. THE ALBUM
SHOULD BE OUT JAN. (87)
NO, SERIOUSLY, THE SHIT
IS SOUNDING REAL GOOD!
THANK GOD FOR ELEPHANT
BEERS. IT MAKES LIFE A LOT
EASIER THESE DAYS.
I BETTER RUN AND
GRAB ONE! AARRGH! LARS x THE GANG

XAVIER RUSSELL
13 LINDE

XAV, YO, WHAT'S
OCCURING??? SITTIN' ON THE
TOURBUS SOMEWHERE IN
KANSAS WATCHING U2 VIDEO
AND WHATEVER ELSE. HOW BE
THINGS IN LONDON.?? WE'VE
BEEN OUT FOR 6 WEEKS W/ WASP
AND A SAINT. AND WASP LEAVE IN
A FEW AND IT'LL JUST BE US
AND SAINT. WE'RE DOIN THE
HOLLYWOOD PALADIUM ON
MARCH 10

SEE YA SOON- LARS X THE GANG !

VIEW FROM THE JOHN HANCOCK CENTER
One of the best views to be seen of Chicago is found at
the John Hancock observatory. As shown, it provides a
spectacular view all its own. Another "must see" for the
Chicago visitor.

Published by Illinois Distributing Co., P.O. Box 1392, Aurora, IL 60507
© Photo by Phil Valdez

XAVIER RUSSELL
13 LINDE

TWO ORIGINAL
"METALLICARDS" SENT
TO CO-AUTHOR RUSSELL.

TOP CARD SENT IN 1986,
DENMARK STUDIO - "MASTER OF PUPPETS".
BOTTOM CARD SENT IN 1985 - ON ROAD WITH
ARMORED SAINT / W.A.S.P. IN AMERICA.

ABOVE: METALLICA TOUR PROGRAMME

METALLICA

JAMES HETFIELD CHURNING OUT
AN "INTENSE" METALLIRIFF.

METALLIFANS GETTING
INTO THE FESTIVAL
SPIRIT, DONINGTON.

CHAPTER TWO

THE MARCH OF THE METAL MILITIA

The true story about Dave Mustaine will never be told, because there's something of a pact between Dave, Metallica and myself.

Johnny Zazula

The first two months of 1983 were probably the most frustrating yet for the screaming infant that was Metallica. Their San Francisco shows and the 'No Life...' demo had aroused quite a tremor on the underground Metal grapevine, but a severe shortage of finance seemed likely to stunt the band's growth at this most crucial stage, castrating the kid before it had even had a chance to enjoy power-chord puberty.

Lars asked Brian Slagel to front $8,000 for the band to record their début album, but as a skint 21-year-old himself, Slagel just didn't have those kind of resources. For a while Metallica moped around the Bay Area desperate for a dollar injection, until one afternoon in March when their friends at the *Metal Mania* fanzine, Ron Quintana and Ian Kallen, told them of a wise-cracking entrepreneurial character on the East Coast who was interested in talking to them and, well, what did they have to lose? Why not give him a call? His name, they were told, was Johnny Zazula.

"My wife Marsha and I were in the record store we owned at the time and we were playing Angel Witch or something, when a customer of ours who'd recently been to California came into the store with the 'No Life Til Leather' demo," recalls Zazula. "Now I didn't really want to be bothered with listening to demos at the time, but we put it on the stereo and within five seconds we both got into it, we really did. I know it sounds crazy and difficult to believe, but before the end of that demo I had visions of Metallica being just what they are today. Don't ask me why, I just knew it.

"Straight after hearing the demo I told Marsha I just had to track the band down, so I contacted the guys who worked for the *Metal Mania* fanzine in Oregon and asked them if they could put me in touch. At the time we were promoting about 12 shows in our area with bands like The Rods, Venom and Vandenberg and I thought Metallica would be such a cool band to add to that bill, so I said to the guys, 'Listen, you've just got to help track this band down'. Lo and behold, Lars called me two days later while I was having my dinner, and straight after our conversation Metallica were on their way... to my house!"

Johnny Z (pronounced Zee), as he likes to be known, was based in New Jersey at the time and in partnership with loving spouse Marsha was trying several small-scale ways of breaking into the music business. Both were big Metal fans, aficionados of the British New Wave, and both saw something in Metallica that they hadn't seen in any of the Metal bands currently working the New York/New Jersey circuit.

Z sent the band $1,500 and they put everything they owned into a U-Haul rental truck and embarked on the week-long crawl across the States. They nearly didn't make it either: a crash with a jeep during a snowstorm near Wyoming left the van's truck in a ditch. No-one was hurt, but as the incident occurred while Dave Mustaine was drink-driving, the others made a mental note that as soon as they started the new phase of their career on the East Coast they had to get rid of him.

"The initial problem though was, when they arrived it was like, 'Oh... now what do we do?'," explains Z. "They had no place to stay, they didn't have a dime in their pockets, they had absolutely nothing. So Marsha and I let them stay at our house for a while and to pay for our food we ran off copies of the 'No Life...' demo on the stereo in our lounge and sold them off for $4.99 each. We actually sold thousands of them, not for profit, just to cover the expense of having four extra mouths to feed."

Not everyone saw Z as the humble benefactor that he presented himself as though, and no sooner had Metallica settled in New Jersey than rumour filtered

VENOM.

over from California that the band had wandered into the craftily woven web of a brazen rip-off merchant. It would be unfair to speculate as to who exactly started spreading those rumours, but suspicion naturally fell on the two people who had a right to feel jealous of Z's magnetism: Brian Slagel at Metal Blade who was naturally quite disappointed that he couldn't hold on to Metallica himself, and Mike Varney, boss of another LA-based indie Metal label called Shrapnel Records, who also attempted to woo the band into his corner.

"There was a lot of rivalry on an East Coast/West Coast level that was really fucked up," rues Z, "and so of course there was all sorts of ugly shit being thrown around when Metallica came to stay with us. To this day I've never really sat down with Brian Slagel or Mike Varney... I guess it was sad what happened. But I was just this guy with a wife who was trying to get something going in a kind of Bill Graham spirit, because he was our idol, and if something like Metallica came my way, of course I was going to hold onto it as hard as I could.

"The situation became so bad that I felt I had to constantly prove myself to the guys, that I could never make one mistake. They were being told that I was a major scumbag, and that the reality of the situation was that I would screw them. In fact, the only reality that Metallica had to face was that I really didn't have much money. But then I must've had something to offer, because both Metal Blade and Shrapnel were going concerns as record companies at the time, and yet the band chose us over both of them."

Johnny Z's problems didn't end there. He soon found himself presiding over the sacking of Dave Mustaine, who'd simply burnt himself out and become a liability in the eyes of his colleagues. Mustaine's last gig with Metallica was on a Saturday night in New York on a bill that also included Venom and Vandenberg. After discussing the matter over a few crates of beer the next day, Hetfield woke the volatile guitarist on the Monday morning to tell him on behalf of the others that he had an hour to pack his things and leave, as they'd booked him on a Greyhound Airlines 'flight' back home. It was a painful decision and the band tried to soften the blow by heading into Manhattan that night and drowning themselves in a bottle of vodka. Nonetheless, it was a decision which had to be made.

He soon found himself presiding over the sacking of Dave Mustaine, who'd simply burnt himself out and become a liability in the eyes of his colleagues. Mustaine's last gig with Metallica was on a Saturday night in New York on a bill that also included Venom and Vandenberg.

TOP: JAMES IN 1983;
BOTTOM: CLIFF IN MID-'PULLING TEETH' MODE.

The first thing they noticed about Kirk Hammett's playing was his very European style: melodic as well as fast and aggressive.

Today Z refuses to elaborate on the events surrounding Mustaine's exit. "The true story about Dave Mustaine will never be told, because there's something of a pact between Dave, Metallica and myself," he says. "All the pain, all the guilt and all the blame came to rest last year, and so now it really is time to let sleeping dogs lie". At the time, however, there wasn't a great deal of love lost between those involved.

"Basically," Mustaine told the *Metal Forces* fanzine shortly after re-emerging with his new band, Megadeth, "when they told me to leave I packed in about 20 seconds and I was gone. I wasn't upset at all as I wanted to start a solo project during the middle of Metallica anyway."

Securing a replacement lead guitarist proved relatively simple. Even before Mustaine had officially been given his marching orders Mark Whittaker, who was now acting as road manager, sound engineer and all-round roadie, had tipped them off about a kid who'd played with a San Francisco Speed Metal band he used to manage called Exodus. In fact, Exodus had even opened for Metallica at the Old Waldorf a few months earlier, and although no-one could actually remember catching the support set that night, Hetfield, Ulrich and Burton were all impressed by the tapes Whittaker played them.

The first thing they noticed about Kirk Hammett's playing was his very European style: melodic as well as fast and aggressive, all attributes he'd picked up under the tutelage of state-of-the-art techno-wizard Joe Satriani, the man who taught Steve Vai among others. Hammett was also a fan of the NWOBHM, although his interest in music went way back to his pre-school days in late sixties San Francisco, and the hippy culture of Jimi Hendrix, The Grateful Dead, Santana and Led Zeppelin.

"Through my brothers and cousins I was around the college crowd, and hippies in general," he says. "They'd take me to street fairs, and I'd get my face painted, have strings of love beads made…"

In short he grew up wanting to be Jimi Hendrix, a notion that took on a more determined slant when he started learning guitar at the age of 15. With his teenage

years came influences from Aerosmith, Thin Lizzy, UFO, ZZ Top and Kiss, and then, ever looking out for new extremes to explore, he discovered punk through The Sex Pistols and realised that you didn't actually have to be a musical genius to get up on a stage and entertain people.

Exodus were actually doing quite well on the Frisco scene when Metallica approached Hammett to join them on the East Coast, but keen to further his career as quickly as possible Kirk didn't linger too long over his reply, even though he initially

KIRK AT LONDON'S MARQUEE IN 1984.

thought the call was an April Fool joke. He arrived in New York after a night flight during April on the same day Mustaine was asked to leave, and while his audition seemed a mere formality he wasn't officially told he'd got the job until talk turned to recording an album.

"At the audition the guys kept smiling at each other," Kirk remembers. "I was like, 'Do they think this is funny? Or are they perpetually happy people?'"

Metallica débuted with Hammett (né Hamster) at the Showplace in New Jersey later in April and then gradually worked him in during a series of NJ club gigs over the next few weeks. When they weren't playing, rehearsals would often stretch to 15-hour days in a pokey Music Building apartment in the New York suburb of Queens, with any spare time spent hanging out with new friends such as local heroes Anthrax, with whom Metallica felt much

> ## At the audition the guys kept smiling at each other. I was like, "Do they think this is funny? Or are they perpetually happy people?"
> ### Kirk Hammett

affinity. In fact, such was the rapport between the two bands, Anthrax guitarist Scott Ian ended up lending Metallica a toaster oven in which the band heated up cheap soup dinners. That was when they weren't in the local Burger King, stealing extra meals by attacking the Eat As Much As U-Like Salad Bar one-by-one using the same plate, thereby only paying for one.

"Anthrax were really the only band on the East Coast who were playing Thrash-type music around this time," says Johnny Z, "so the two bands took to one another straight away. Anthrax were a bunch of kids who were everywhere in those days, they'd show up at every gig, every party, every function… I mean, I'd go to the bathroom to take a piss and they'd be right there behind me! But they were so keen they used to do everything they could to help both me and Metallica - and if that meant lending them equipment, buying them meals, doing anything they could, then so be it. We all kind of worked together."

Z the visionary had taken both bands (as well as Raven) under the wing of his Crazed Management company at this point and was planning a triple-pronged attempt at World Domination from his own sitting room. As far as Metallica were concerned that would first mean getting an album recorded, and so the Zs mustered up all the money they could from their record store business and set the band to work during May at Music America Recording Studios in Rochester, in upstate New York, with the owner of the place Paul Curcio (who also claimed to have discovered Journey guitarist Neal Schon) acting as producer.

"Joey DeMaio from Manowar (with whom Z also worked) told me about the studio," he explains. "It was in the basement of this old colonial-type of club, but there was a huge old ballroom on the second floor that Joey said would be great for getting a drum sound. I knew how fussy Lars was about his drum sound so I flew up to Rochester just to check out this room, that's how much care we took over the album."

The band actually spent six weeks recording the album, costing Z "somewhere in the region of $12-15,000". It

JAMES IN NOTORIOUS MUYA T-SHIRT.

kindred spirit in the UK called Steve Mason, whose London-based Music For Nations label had been launched earlier in the year with a release by New York's Virgin Steele.

"Those guys were a real lifeline," says Z, "and I have to thank them both for giving me a shot because I was a real unknown back then. You really have to give them credit for having the vision to get in on the Metallica thing at a time when a lot of people thought the band were a joke. Without their support, perhaps we'd never have gotten the band off the ground."

Z worked out deals with both Relativity (for distribution in the States) and Music For Nations (for releasing the album in Europe) and finalised the presentation of the first Metallica album during the early summer of 1983. The original title of the album was 'Metal Up Your Ass' - a phrase Lars claimed to have invented "one evening when I was wasted" - and artwork illustrating that very legend showing an arm sprouting from a toilet holding a machete was drawn up

The words of 'Whiplash', meanwhile, simply spoke for themselves: '...Bang your head against the seat/Like you never did before/Make it ring, make it bleed/Make it really sore...'

One head that was permanently sore was that of Bay Area 'Banger and band mascot Rich Birch, who was thought to have inspired the lyrics to 'Whiplash', which in turn led to the now infamous quote on the back sleeve of the album: 'Bang that head that doesn't bang'.

The photograph on that back sleeve also illustrates just how young the band were then, too: spotty, barely-shaven faces, pessimistic haircuts and particularly dodgy HM attire were very much the order of the day.

In America 'Kill 'Em All', according to a relieved Johnny Z, "sold about 7,000 copies straight out of the box, which was really exciting. In the greater scheme of things it wasn't the biggest album in the world - in fact, the second album which we released on Megaforce, 'All For One' by Raven, sold much more than the first Metallica album - but at least it proved to us that there was a market out there for the kind of music Metallica were coming out with."

Indeed, across the water in the UK the band were making possibly the biggest impact on the underground

The original title of the album was 'Metal Up Your Ass' - a phrase Lars claimed to have invented "one evening when I was wasted" - and artwork illustrating that very legend showing an arm sprouting from a toilet holding a machete was drawn up expectantly.

was a lot more than he wanted to spend, but once both he and Marsha had committed themselves to the project they found they couldn't really get out of going the whole hog.

"Marsha and I put ourselves in a lot of debt to make that album, we really took a chance with our lives," says Z. "Every penny we made from the store would be sent straight up to the studio to keep the recording process rolling, and yet when it was finished we found there was hardly anyone interested in putting it out. We sat down with a lot of A&R people, but nobody really understood what was going on here. We didn't want to start a record company of our own at all, but we ended up putting the record out on our own because of the lack of interest elsewhere."

The Z's response to such lethargy was Megaforce Records, an independent New Jersey-based operation which would soon burgeon into one of the most fruitful and influential Metal labels in the world, but which at the time of Metallica's first album was a real shot-in-the-dark one-off. With bated breath Z shopped around for the vital distribution deal, and while many dismissed him as an amateur dabbling in a cut-throat business which was bound to burn him, he did find sympathetic support from Barry Coburn who owned the Relativity company in the States, and a

expectantly. As the release date loomed however, Relativity felt the whole thing was a little too risqué and Z suggested the band came up with an alternative concept.

"So we got our own back by saying 'Kill 'Em All'," Lars explained at the time, "and that title kinda stuck."

Featuring an equally gruesome cover which depicted a sledgehammer lying in a pool of blood, 'Kill 'Em All' was released in July 1983 to a mixed reception from press and punters alike. Some hailed it as the future of Metal, some as the very worst example of the genre; either way it got a gut reaction.

The essence of the album was its ferocious speed and uncouth power. Most of the tracks from the 'No Life...' demo had been reproduced with double the intensity, especially 'Motorbreath' and 'Metal Militia' which seemed to set the speed-of-light standard for all future perpetrators of Thrash, while others like 'The Four Horsemen' (a retitled version of 'Mechanix') and 'No Remorse' sounded like two juggernauts colliding in an echo chamber.

Metal scene since Iron Maiden in the halcyon days of the NWOBHM, sweeping the 1983 polls in fanzines like *Metal Forces*, where they were voted Best Band, with 'Kill 'Em All' Best Album and Kirk Hammett Best Guitarist - even though a bitter Dave Mustaine later contested the legitimacy of that choice, complaining that, "Kirk got a free ride to number one because of my guitar solos from the 'No Life Til Leather' demo".

The first single from the album, 'Jump In The Fire', is also worth a mention, if only for the hell of disclosing for the first time that the two tracks slapped on the B-side, 'Seek And Destroy' and 'Phantom Lord', which were supposed to have been recorded live, were actually recorded in an American studio on October 24 and remixed by Music For Nations using overdubbed applause from a Twelfth Night show at the Marquee! Metallica fans might find that hard to believe, but it's true... yes, Twelfth Night must have been applauded at some point.

Back in the States none of the impact

of 'Kill 'Em All' had been lost on the enthusiastic souls behind Crazed Management and Megaforce Records. Encouraged by the successful start of both punts, Z put Raven (who despite being considered a joke in the UK were actually making waves in the US) and Metallica together for a 36-show coast-to-coast tour that would stretch throughout the rest of the American summer, climaxing somewhat inevitably at The Stone in San Francisco. In his own words the so-called 'Kill 'Em All For One' tour (geddit?) "was a real slog, a shoestring budget, hardship right along the line, and not one for the faint-hearted. It wasn't a record-breaking tour attendance-wise, but it certainly got its point across, and it was the first of its kind in a way because there were no promoters involved, no agents involved, no PR people involved... just me and a guy named John Ditmar on the phone hassling people! By the time we got home Metallica were huge in our area, which was

incredible if you consider the scale on which everything was done."

The Metallica assault on the rest of the world, however, was experiencing a number of niggling delays. Plans had been laid during September for a double-header UK tour with Megaforce labelmates Manowar, and a Japanese tour with Tokyo terrors Loudness was also mooted at one stage, but never realised. The band were destined to spend the rest of the year in America demoing ideas for their second album.

In the end Metallica's first show on foreign territory was pencilled in for February 3, 1984, at the Volkshaus in Zurich, Switzerland, opening for Geordie jesters Venom on what became known infamously as the 'Seven Dates Of Hell' tour. The trek actually consisted of six rather modest European appointments with a day off in between, and then a nine month gap before the last one at Hammersmith Odeon in London (which Metallica never

appeared at anyway), but nevertheless it was to be the band's grand introduction to the European Metal fans who'd so far shown considerable interest in Metallica on an underground level.

"Metallica had a huge underground following by this time," says Gem Howard, who worked as the band's tour manager on that inaugural foray. "It was all down to the tape-exchange system that goes on; the 'No Life...' demo had gone around everywhere, picking up coverage from fanzines like *Scum* and *Disaster* and causing a real groundswell of interest. The kids who're into that kind of stuff become part of a massive network, they spend all their time swapping tapes and stuff, and therefore any band that gets into that system gets a very credible name for itself.

"Now the thing that Metallica had which really worked for them was the name. That name just summed up what they were all about, and I'm sure that attracted a lot of kids to them. Nobody seeing the name

METALLICA, CIRCA 1983, LEFT TO RIGHT:
KIRK HAMMETT, JAMES HETFIELD, LARS ULRICH AND CLIFF BURTON.

Indeed, those who witnessed the 'Seven-ish Dates Of Hell' tour generally agreed that Metallica came out on top of headliners Venom, who never really had the intrinsic expertise to make it as a real, professional, performing unit.

Metallica could have been in any doubt about what the music sounded like, so the kids knew what they were getting before they even bought the album."

Gem had first heard the album when he got a call from an ex-colleague called Martin Hooker, who he'd worked with at the independent Secret Records in the Seventies, but who'd now begun to establish Music For Nations with Steve Mason. Hooker asked Howard if he'd be prepared to tour manage an American band who were coming to Europe for the first time, and not having anything better to do at the time, he agreed.

"When Martin gave me a copy of 'Kill 'Em All' I thought it was... different," he considers, "especially from the stuff that was around at the time. But it didn't completely knock me out and make me think it was the future of rock. In fact, if someone had told me at any point during the first couple of tours we did that this band was going to have a number one album I'd have told them they were mad, because it just wasn't the kind of music I thought had enough crossover appeal to achieve that kind of success. I mean, I'd always worked within the indie market and knew from experience that anything could happen; I worked with The Exploited when they did *Top Of The Pops*, so I knew miracles were possible! But as far as Metallica were concerned... I just couldn't see this tremendous racket getting to the top of the charts, and to be perfectly honest I don't think they could either.

"There was something slightly more to Metallica than first met the ear though. Punk was just 'DADADADADADADADA' kind of thing, a mindless noise that didn't really go anywhere. But Metallica had something which actually was musical in its own way. There were those 'chugga-chugga-chugga' guitars in there and it was pretty fast stuff, but the band also seemed to be trying to throw some pretty weird bits in there as well, and that made me slightly intrigued by them. Beneath the noise they were actually quite good."

Indeed, those who witnessed the 'Seven-ish Dates Of Hell' tour generally agreed that Metallica came out on top of headliners Venom, who despite being pioneers of the Thrash genre and having a couple of pace-setting albums under their bullet-belts, never really had the intrinsic expertise to make it as a real, professional, performing unit. Metallica were still very much spotty teens charging heads-down through the mêlée themselves at this juncture, masking what they lacked in true musical ability with abstract torrents of high-decibel delirium. But they did seem to have something more than the hype which preceded Cronos, Mantas and Abaddon, the crackpot components of Venom, and the Thrash connoisseurs of the Continent seemed to revel in their discovery.

After Zurich the tour crashed through Milan, Nuremburg and Paris before finishing at Poperinge on the Belgian-French border on February 12. But the most significant show of the tour was at the Aardschok Festival at Ijsselhal in Zwolle, Holland the previous day, an event which traditionally brought together the soured cream of Europe's underground Metal scene, a sort of low-budget, bargain-bin Donington.

The 1984 blow-out featured Horizon, Savage and Tokyo Blade as well as Metallica and Venom, all huddled together in a hall that resembled an old aircraft hangar, and detailing his thoughts in the crucial *Kerrang!* review co-author Russell (who also got roped into introducing the band on stage) insisted that Metallica took the honours - which was just as well considering this particular performance became one of the most sought after Metallica bootlegs, and is currently available in a number of different formats.

Naturally the band's set at this stage was essentially 'Kill 'Em All' revisited. An intro tape of 'For A Few Dollars More' (the first sign of soundtrack composer Ennio Morricone's influence on the band's music) led them into the fray, before 'Hit The

Lights', 'The Four Horsemen', 'Jump In The Fire', 'Phantom Lord', 'Motorbreath', 'Seek And Destroy' and 'Whiplash' were sped through like the band were being paid by the song. The only distractions from the blur were Cliff Burton's eccentric bass solo, aptly dubbed 'Pulling Teeth', in which he headbanged in a frenzied rotating motion like a Dutch windmill in a hurricane, and a new track entitled 'Ride The Lightning', which Hetfield explained was about the use of the electric chair in America, and which felt like it too.

Metallica wrapped up their 90 minutes by encoring with 'Metal Militia', during which the locals were encouraged to chant 'Metal Up Your Ass', and then they were gone, leaving Venom to pick up the pieces and climax the evening with more blood-curdling dementia.

"Metallica knew what Aardschok meant," says Gem, "and they really worked towards that festival. They knew that success at that show would mean them making a big name for themselves in Holland, and would even go a long way towards establishing them in Europe as a whole. Fortunately the show was a real stormer - 6,000 kids going absolutely crazy, which was unbelievable to see - and we came away from Holland feeling we'd really taken a big stride towards breaking the band.

"In fact, the buzz on Metallica was such that we went back to Johnny Z at this point and asked him to do another album with us. Z said he had the band under contract for another album but that he couldn't afford to record it. So we agreed to pay for another album to be done on the condition that we also got a contract for the third."

The day after the Venom tour ended, February 13, Metallica flew up to Copenhagen in Denmark to start work on the second album. They'd chosen Sweet Silence Studios - once again partly because of the drum sound Lars thought he could get from one of the huge attic-type rooms at the complex, and partly because it gave Lars the chance to act the proud native - and they'd also decided to entrust production to SS's resident engineer Flemming Rasmusson, who'd worked on Rainbow's 'Bent Out Of Shape' album the previous

Metallica wrapped up their 90 minutes by encoring with 'Metal Militia', during which the locals were encouraged to chant 'Metal Up Your Ass'.

JAMES AND KIRK ON STAGE AT THE
MARQUEE, APRIL 1984.

year, and had also tampered with Denmark's very own underground Metal demons, Mercyful Fate.

Once again, though, rumours abounded about Metallica's stability, with some whispers suggesting that Lars was about to be replaced by Slayer's Dave Lombardo and that James wanted to relinquish his role as frontman and retire to the less stressful art of the rhythm guitar.

"There didn't seem to be much truth in the Dave Lombardo story," says Gem, "but James was quite insistent on having a frontman singer in the band for the new album, because he felt he wasn't doing a very good job. Johnny Z asked John Bush

At the end of the day I think James agreed that while he wasn't the best singer in the world, his vocal style did fit in with the lyrics he was coming up with – like, Metallica don't write love songs, right?

from Armored Saint to join the band again, but like before Bush felt he had to stick with his mates in the Saint, and so James had to reconsider his position, because there wasn't really anybody else the band wanted as lead singer.

"At the end of the day I think James agreed that while he wasn't the best singer in the world, his vocal style did fit in with the lyrics he was coming up with - like, Metallica don't write love songs, right? - and that there was a certain strangeness to his voice that added some authenticity to the themes the band were working around. James wrote most of the lyrics anyway, and when you get singers singing someone else's lyrics, you tend to get a sort of 'going through the motions' vibe. At least with James singing you had a touch of originality in there."

"Metallica is Metallica," John Bush was to state later, "and James Hetfield is the natural frontman for that band. I must say I was very surprised when they asked me... I seriously thought about their offer, but deep down I knew my voice wasn't right for their material. Anyway, as far as Armored Saint are concerned, we've known each other for years and it's like my natural home. If I were to leave that band I'd be in the gutter. Yet strange as it may seem, Metallica is the only other band I'd feel comfortable in."

Ever stranger would be the fact that Bush was to later join Metallica's rivals, Anthrax!

For the time being though, the Metallica line-up remained the same. But as work on the album progressed, financial pressures started to weigh heavily on them and give Lars, in particular, concern for the stability of the band's external support system, a situation which led to disruptive influences outside the Megaforce/Music For Nations axis attempting to wrestle control of the project.

"We were pretty broke at the time," Johnny Z admits, "mainly because we got ripped off by our distributor in a major, major way. It was only later that we realised exactly how much we were ripped off for, but at the time all we knew was that Metallica was doing real well and yet we weren't seeing the kind of money we should've been seeing.

"All this was happening while the band were in Copenhagen, and after a while things started to happen which made everyone feel a little uneasy. Although the budget for the album was supposed to be about $20,000, already it had gone up to something like $30,000, and still it wasn't finished. So I was on the phone saying, 'Hey guys, what are you doing? Who the fuck's gonna pay for all this?' And Lars was on the other end of the line going, 'Hey, who can say how much a record is gonna cost? When the record is done, it's done'. It went on like that and we ended up having a few heated exchanges."

In the meantime Gerry Bron, head of the Bron organisation which owned Bronze Records (home of Metallica faves Motörhead), had taken a big interest in Metallica and had flown out to Copenhagen to coax them into signing both a management and US record deal. Arriving after the band had simply laid down the basic tracks, he immediately made himself unpopular by suggesting that if the album was to be released on Bronze in America it would have to be remixed by renowned producer/engineer Eddie Kramer, but having been seduced by the money he might front them, Lars and the others reluctantly agreed to many of his

The 'Hell On Earth' tour was announced at the end of February, to commence on March 21 at Hanley Victoria Hall in Stoke-On-Trent.

original stipulations.

Johnny Z, meanwhile, flew to Europe to try to sort out the whole mess, naturally hoping to protect his own interests as well as those of his band. It proved a shattering experience which effectively loosened his grip on Metallica.

"It was my first time abroad and I was just eaten up," he admits dejectedly. "I was Bambi in a forest full of hunters - all these English businessmen with their pots and pots of money, and me running up debts I didn't even know I could pay. Not only had the album cost much more than it was supposed to, but the band had blown all of their European money on the Venom tour, so I was going, 'Whooooaaaah, this is getting out of hand!'

"Of course by this time the band had all sorts of people whispering in their ears - 'Hey, I can do this for you!', 'Hey, why don't you come with me?' - and it was really getting me down. In the end I sat down with Gerry Bron to try to come to some arrangement, but it quickly became obvious it wasn't going to work.

Gerry let his son Richard get involved with it all and that was a big mistake, because in my opinion that guy was just a dickhead, and I told him so. I mean, Caligula Junior, or what? I just couldn't work with that guy at all, so the whole Bronze thing fell apart."

The upshot of all the confusion was that Metallica decided to stick with Crazed Management for America and Music For Nations in Europe for the present, and simply look for a new label in the US and new management for Europe. In the meantime the new album, 'Ride The Lightning', was ready to roll in Europe, so the band dossed in London while the Music For Nations think tank considered a plan of action which would finally introduce Metallica to the British public.

As the Metallica deal with Megaforce also included The Rods and Exciter (as well as Anthrax) both Z and MFN agreed that a package of the three bands might be the best way to proceed. Thus, in conjunction with Birmingham-based promoters MCP, the 'Hell On Earth' tour was announced at the end of February, to commence on

March 21 at Hanley Victoria Hall in Stoke-On-Trent.

In the weeks that followed the announcement MFN worked with *Kerrang!* - at the time the only British magazine devoted to Heavy Metal - to promote the tour, even offering a cut-out coupon which entitled the bearer to £1.00 off the face value of a ticket to any of the 'Hell On Earth' shows. However, the venues booked for the tour - Hammersmith Odeon, Manchester Apollo, Birmingham Odeon and the like - did seem a little over ambitious for three bands who'd yet to break the UK market, and as the opening night grew nearer panic began to set in amongst the organisers.

"About two weeks before the start of the tour we noticed to our dismay that our best-selling show was the Newcastle Mayfair," recalls Gem, "where we'd sold a massive 14 tickets. It was at that moment that we thought the tour might not be the success we wanted it to be, so we cancelled it immediately. It was very embarrassing, even more so when you consider that the band had flown into Britain from Denmark at this point and were fully expecting to steam straight into the tour!"

In the end the band spent their spare time hanging out in London with their friends from Anthrax, in town to promote their 'Fistful Of Metal' album. One incident during this time worth recalling was told later to *Kerrang!* by Anthrax guitarist Scott Ian.

"One day Cliff (Burton) and I were heading to Tottenham Court Road by tube to go shopping as Cliff needed a new Walkman. We got into the underground station and there was a lot of police patrolling about. As we stood there waiting for the train, two policemen approached us and said, 'If we were to search you right now, would we find any drugs?' And being the smart Americans that we are, we said, 'No'.

"Well, they didn't believe our simple 'No' and told us we were under arrest on suspicion of possibly carrying something illegal. They took the pair of us to a police station and locked us in a room with no windows. We just sat there and waited. I was worried about getting out and Cliff was pissed off because it was his only day to go shopping. Two different policemen came in and stripped us down to our underwear. They proceeded to search everywhere. Of course, they didn't find anything illegal, but what they did find were Cliff's allergy and cold pills. Cliff tried to explain that it was just cold medicine but they wouldn't listen. They must have been thinking of the big raises and promotions they would get for busting these two long-haired American drug kingpins. They said they'd have to send the pills to the lab to be tested and that we'd have to wait; they also said they were going to take Cliff back to the flat to search the place for more pills.

"It turns out, they went back to the flat, searched the place - surprising Kirk who was playing the guitar when Cliff walks in with six cops - but they didn't find anything. The lab told them their big narcotics bust was only a phlegm expectorant and that they would have to let us go.

"The captain called us into his office and apologised; he said that in America we'd probably have been treated even worse. Cliff told him that in America the police don't stop you for having long hair and that most US cops can tell the difference between a cold pill and a Quaalude, and that they spend their time tracking down real lawbreakers like jaywalkers. So we left on that note - before they could think of anything else to charge us with..."

In the meantime Music For Nations were desperately trying to arrange a London gig to officially introduce their American acquisitions to the British Thrash fraternity. After hasty negotiations they came up with a one-off show at London's Marquee Club for Metallica, and another one-off for Exciter at the Royal Standard pub in Walthamstow in east London. And so it was that, after six months of waiting, Metallica finally made their UK début on March 27 within the gloomy confines of the Wardour Street watering hole, the scene of many an historic rock'n'roll night since its heyday in the Swinging Sixties.

The show itself was mostly culled from the 'Kill 'Em All' album, rounded out with several snippets from the forthcoming

'Ride The Lightning' like 'For Whom The Bell Tolls', 'Fight Fire With Fire' and 'Creeping Death'. Afterwards, in high spirits, Hetfield and Ulrich hit the town for a celebratory rave-up, starting at the nearby Wardour Street pub, The Ship, then predictably staggering across the road to the sleaze-pit St. Moritz Club, before agreeing to crash the night at the Notting Hill Gate pad of co-author Russell.

However, the mixture of several litres of Rebel Yell Bourbon with an hour or two of headbanging and 'air guitar' playing to Riot, Blue Öyster Cult and Molly Hatchet eventually took its toll, and both James and Lars ended up vomiting wildly into the giant bucket of Kentucky Fried chicken legs they'd bought earlier, filling it to the brim. The evening finally ended with neighbours calling the police at 5.00am, and Russell smuggling the extremely drunken twosome back to their Bayswater flat.

After another suitably lively Ship/St. Moritz session, Hetfield was seen to

Marquee, this time before the keen eyes of Bronze, who'd been down to watch the band rehearse in West Kensington and were still clinging to the idea of signing them. If anything, the show was better than the previous one, but by now the whole Bronze idea had been swept under the carpet,

amounts of Carlsberg Elephant lager and, possibly, finish off 'Ride The Lightning'. By now they'd cultivated quite a reputation as 'enthusiastic' drinkers and nomadic urchins, hanging out with anyone who offered to buy them a beer and indulging in all the usual 'boys-on- vacation' pranks. Those who ran with the band during these early days remember the unashamed laddishness of it all with some affection.

"The band were staying in a tiny flat near Queensway in West London which we'd rented for them," says Gem Howard, "and although we used

The mixture of several litres of Rebel Yell Bourbon with an hour or two of headbanging and 'air guitar' playing to Riot, Blue Öyster Cult and Molly Hatchet eventually took its toll, and both James and Lars ended up vomiting wildly into the giant bucket of Kentucky Fried chicken legs.

stumble along Oxford Street looking for mischief, eventually climbing on to the roof of the Classic Cannon cinema and, for reasons best known to himself, attempting to dismantle the building's large neon sign. Needless to say this particular escapade culminated in his being led off to the slammer by several unamused policemen, later to be released with a severe warning.

Almost two weeks later, on April 8, Metallica played their second show at The

and the band simply concentrated on winning over the fans who'd turned up after the word-of-mouth buzz created by the first show.

After the Marquee shows Metallica flew back to Copenhagen to drink copious

to do that kind of thing a lot for our acts I can claim without fear of contradiction that none were filthier than Metallica. I walked in one day and the smell nearly knocked me over. Every bit of crockery in their kitchen had been used, so they'd been eating off dirty plates because no one could be bothered to do the washing up. I even saw one of them eating cereal from a mixing bowl one day, simply because it was the only thing left unused.

"In the lounge there was a glass coffee table with pieces of glass on the floor... a mass of butter which had obviously been dropped by someone and trodden into the carpet by everyone else... bits of paper strewn all around the room... empty beer cans down the side of the furniture... crap everywhere. It was disgusting."

Nevertheless the spirit in Metallica during these formative days was probably at an all time high, something which could never be recaptured, as Gem came to realise when he took them back on the road in Europe during June to open for

TWISTED SISTER.

Twisted Sister, the made-up madmen from New York whose 'Under The Blade' début had appeared on Secret Records back in 1982.

"We did five dates with Twisted Sister - even closing one show in Zwaagwesteinde, Northern Holland, because Metallica were more popular than Twisted Sister in that area - and the camaraderie was great, real 'lads on the road' stuff. I remember having a good laugh doing simple things like driving overnight in our tiny minibus to silly little hotels in odd-sounding Belgian towns, and working so close to the band as a tour manager that I got to know the different personalities in a very short space of time.

"For a start they all seemed to have varied interests in music: Lars was into the

"Cliff was also the one who would usually be out drinking and chatting with whoever was around, unlike James who was very quiet and would hardly speak at all. Kirk was also fairly quiet - until he'd knock on your hotel room door at 4.00am and want to talk about guitar strings or something - and while Lars would talk and talk and talk, he really was quite serious most of the time, wanting to know about the business side of things. He's not the kind of guy who tells jokes.

"Overall, Metallica weren't the kind of band who went too wild on the road - they didn't wreck hotel rooms or any of the clichéd stuff - but occasionally James or someone would get too pissed and I'd have to take him to the hospital to get his hand

Now Metallica had Kirk there weren't as many ego problems, so James just let Cliff carry the visual side of things

NWOBHM, James was into GBH, Discharge and the slightly harder stuff, Kirk was into all sorts of things, and Cliff would sit in the front of the van playing The Misfits - banging the crap out of the dashboard with his fists - before putting on something like 'Homeward Bound' by Simon & Garfunkel! He was also a big fan of Southern Rock, especially Lynyrd Skynyrd, and in fact he often tried to persuade the rest of the guys to cover 'Freebird'!

"But then Cliff was different from the rest, right down to the way he used to dress. The image of the band was real street-level stuff - jeans, T-shirts and trainers - but Cliff would probably be wearing an olive-green grandad-shirt and bell-bottomed loon pants! He was the son of two San Francisco hippies and he still had those hippy ideals; he liked his beer, liked his pot or whatever, liked to chill out, and he was really laid-back, relaxed and happy. His sense of humour was great, as were his bass solos and everything about his stage presence. In fact, although he was pretty cool offstage, when he got onstage he would just go wild - headbanging out of time and throwing everyone else out of time as well! He was the most visual of all the band onstage, particularly as James had become a bit more laid-back since Dave Mustaine had left the band. James was wild when Mustaine was next to him because Mustaine would try to push James to the back all the time, but now Metallica had Kirk there weren't as many ego problems, so James just let Cliff carry the visual side of things.

stitched up or something. Also, I do remember the 'On The Road' photo book which they kept, full of pictures of 'obliging' female fans in the most outrageous positions... none of which could possibly be published in a book of this sort!

"So there was some high jinx from time to time, with lots of beer and vodka drunk, and like most bands there was some dabbling in the odd line of cocaine that would come round. But in general they didn't live for drugs and chicks and the typical rock'n'roll lifestyle, they were more interested in getting on with the music, because that's what they were there for."

When the Twisted Sister tour was completed with what is generally remembered as a lacklustre third-on-the-bill appearance at the Heavy Sound Festival in Poperinge, Belgium, on June 10 - on a bill that also included in reverse order H-Bomb, Faithful Breath, Lita Ford, Mercyful Fate, Baron Rojo and headliners Motörhead - Metallica returned to London to await the July release of 'Ride The Lightning' with much anticipation. It was perhaps the end of a chapter of innocence, as the new campaign would involve their being heaved on to a higher rung by the ruthless forces of big business, and the band would leave behind in their wake many of those who strove to make it happen for them in first place.

Metallica were about to 'Ride The Lightning' into a whole new territory, and only the rich would survive.

CHAPTER THREE

LIGHTNING STRIKES

'Ride The Lightning' was finally released on the Music For Nations label in Europe on July 27, 1984, entering the UK album charts the following month at a respectable 87. In the US it hit the stores on Megaforce and in the words of Johnny Z "flew out of the box" just as fast, although once again critical opinion of the album was mixed.

Lars in particular had developed an opinion that if Metallica were really going to be big they'd have to sign with a powerful management company and a major record label, and soon.

Even as early as their second album Metallica faced accusations of 'selling out', of betraying the Thrashier Than Thou promises of their début and unacceptably slowing down their approach. Put another way, this meant that the band were actually learning to play a bit better, write a bit better and structure their works in a way which didn't necessitate everything degenerating into a white-noise blur.

Metallica were still basking in the burning-rubber heat of Thrash ideals, make no mistake: opening cut 'Fight Fire With Fire', 'Trapped Under Ice' (originally called 'When Hell Freezes Over') and 'Creeping Death' rocketed through at a scorching pace, proving the band could show a clean pair of heels to most of their contemporaries. But the epic instrumental 'Call Of Ktulu' (like the title track, co-written by Dave Mustaine), the brooding 'Fade To Black' and the lighter, dare-anybody-say-it, almost 'radio-friendly' 'Escape', illustrated how Metallica were sensing the chance to broaden their creative horizons and mature into a multi-dimensional relative of the terms of the songs, the production and the performance, this LP is far superior than anything we've ever recorded. There's a lot more melody in 'Ride The Lightning' material; the choruses are more out in the open and the arrangements are much better."

"'Ride The Lightning' is not like one complete track like 'Kill 'Em All' was," said Ulrich, "because then all the tracks were played at 'Metal Militia' speed. You see, the one thing we realised between making 'Kill 'Em All' and 'Ride The Lightning' was that you don't have to depend on speed to be powerful and heavy - I think songs like 'For Whom The Bell Tolls' and 'Ride The Lightning' reflect that sort of attitude.

"OK, there's always the odd letter or comment like, 'If you don't play ten 'Metal Militias' on every album then it's not Metallica and it's not good', but we're doing what we're doing the way we feel at a certain time. The band has matured and we're still learning. If people think we're wimping out then fuck 'em, we don't need that kinda shit."

Generally, however, Metallica's real fans were right behind them, and a lucky few were repaid by a secret gig at a run-down punk club called Mabuhay Gardens in San Francisco during June, where Hetfield, Burton, Hammett and Ulrich became The Four Horsemen for the night. Metallica also had the power of the press in their back pocket - gaining yet more rave reviews in Europe after their appearance at the Breaking Sound Festival at Le Bourget in Paris on August 29. They eventually returned to America at the end of the summer for a one-off date with Raven, content in the knowledge that 'Ride The Lightning' had sold some 85,000 copies.

In the States the record made encouraging progress as well, but the highly business-minded Lars in particular had developed an opinion that if Metallica were really going to be big they'd have to sign with a powerful management company and a major record label, and soon.

"We'd sold 75,000 copies of 'Ride The Lightning' in the States," says Johnny Z, "which was unheard of for an indie label, absolutely incredible. So I kept saying to them, 'Hang on in there guys, we'll pull through'. But at the time I just didn't have

the money they wanted, I didn't have a penny left - in fact if you look at the credits in 'Ride The Lightning' you'll see they call me Johnny 'The Well Is Dry' Z, because that was my catch phrase at the time - and so I could understand why they wanted to go with a more stable management and record company.

"All the time the vibe between us was getting worse and worse, which was a great shame because we'd done an incredible job together and I felt it would've only got better.

> **"'Ride The Lightning' is not like one complete track like 'Kill 'Em All' was, because then all the tracks were played at 'Metal Militia' speed. You see, the one thing we realised between making 'Kill 'Em All' and 'Ride The Lightning' was that you don't have to depend on speed to be powerful and heavy – I think songs like 'For Whom The Bell Tolls' and 'Ride The Lightning' reflect that sort of attitude."**
>
> **Lars Ulrich**

I mean, it would've been a multi-million dollar job for a major label to get the band where we'd got them on virtually nothing. But I guess the band felt they had to make a decision which would allow them to further their career. They just didn't want to take any risks any more, and, of course, by this time their minds had been poisoned by the people who wanted their asses. It was a horrible, horrible situation to be in at the time, but looking back I guess you can say it worked out best for both of us, because Metallica went on to become a huge band, and we went on to make lots of money out of it."

At the show with Raven at The Roseland Ballroom in New York City, Metallica were watched by, amongst others, representative vultures from the heavyweight organisations like Elektra Records, the ATI booking agency (who looked after Kiss, Iron Maiden and Def Leppard) and Q-Prime Inc. Management, who handled the affairs of Def Leppard, Dokken and Metallica's close friends, Armored Saint. And even though Lars

claimed, "It was one of the worst gigs we've ever done", contracts with all three organisations were signed within weeks.

Initially, however, Q-Prime had a problem contacting Metallica. They knew they'd gone back to San Francisco, but were having trouble locating them. In desperation Q-Prime's Peter Mensch called the Kerrang! offices in London for help, and while no-one could offer him a number for the band's house, co-author Russell told Mensch he could probably get in touch with Kirk Hammett's mother and pass on a message. This was duly done, and Mrs. Hammett immediately whizzed round on a skateboard to 3132 Carlson Boulevard with the news of Q-Prime's interest. Minutes later Lars reversed the charges from a nearby phone-box to the Kerrang! office, Mensch's number was passed on to him there and then, and legend has it the deal was done in that very phone booth. Phase Two of Metallica's career was about to kick.

Not that this transitional period for Metallica passed without throwing up yet more controversy. The callous single-mindedness with which Q-Prime bosses Peter Mensch and Cliff Burnstein pursued the band sowed the seeds of several vicious (and who knows, possibly accurate) rumours. And Elektra became embroiled in a bloody dog-fight with four other major labels in their attempt to win the band's attentions: some stories surrounding the Elektra deal even went as far as to suggest depraved homosexual activities between James Hetfield and Elektra A&R man Michael Alago. It must be stressed that neither the authors nor the publishers have any tangible evidence to confirm any truth in that particular rumour, and therefore conclude that it must simply have been the result of malicious, unfounded gossip.

While Elektra repackaged 'Ride The Lightning' in preparation for a re-release in the States, Metallica returned to Europe to promote the album with a twenty-odd date bout of shows across Belgium, France, Italy, Switzerland, Germany, Holland, Denmark, Sweden, Finland and England, destined to take them right up to Christmas. Music For Nations marked the occasion by releasing 'Creeping Death' as

create a rather disturbing effect every time he went to sing (when James eventually sussed the set-up he completely threw the rest of the song!); not to mention the time in Germany when Tony the lighting engineer and guitar roadie Andy Battye drank three bottles of tequila between them at a seedy nightclub and returned to the tour bus in a semi-comatose stupor to crash out, whereupon the former mistook Kirk Hammett's bunk for the toilet and relieved himself all over the snoozing and 'slightly miffed' guitarist.

The New Year began on a sour note for Metallica, however, as American news agencies crackled with curiosity over a murder story involving the band's name. As the facts became clear it transpired that a couple of 18-year-old kids high on acid had been cruising to Corpus Christi in Texas from San Antonio when they'd picked up a hitch-hiker, who they later tried to rob.

When the reluctant passenger jumped clear from the car, the would-be wallet-snatchers pursued their prey in earnest, one of them eventually

a 12" EP single, as well as a limited edition picture disc, on November 23, and those who shelled out for it found Metallicised versions of Diamond Head's 'Am I Evil?' and Blitzkrieg's 'Blitzkrieg' on the B-side.

"Well," explained Lars, "HM record companies in Europe prefer to have 'Unavailable anywhere else' type shit on the B-side of singles. Now, we're not a band who likes to submit our own songs for B-sides because we like to have them on albums, so we just went into the studio and knocked out a couple of cover songs. They're the only two cover songs that we still play at rehearsals, or live for the seventh encore!"

The band's love for Diamond Head had always been well documented, but what about the lesser-known Blitzkrieg, the Leicester-based outfit who'd been signed to Neat Records during the early '80s? Again this was another example of Lars' obsession with the NWOBHM, and while some members of the now-defunct band weren't aware of Metallica's intentions at the time, they later commended the version of their title song which appeared on the 'Creeping Death' EP (and, no doubt, gratefully accepted the royalties that arrived thereafter).

"The first I heard about it," guitarist Ian Jones said later, "was when my dad, who buys and sells records, phoned up and said 'Hey, I've just come across a band called Metallica who've covered your song!' I didn't believe him at first, I thought he was winding me up. But when I finally heard the record I said to myself, 'Wow, this is serious stuff!' I have to honestly say that I preferred their version to ours."

"Although many of our lyrics deal with violence and death," James Hetfield explained carefully, "we don't try to promote it."

By way of a 'thank you' Metallica flew Jones out to Paris to see them play the following year, conspiring to get their guest completely drunk before inviting him along to a transvestite nightclub as part of a typical band wind-up. The two parties later became good friends, and by way of returning the compliment Jones included a 30-second burst of 'Creeping Death' on his solo album 'Dead Easy', recorded with the help of Diamond Head's Brian Tatler.

"I asked Lars what he thought of it," says Jones, "and he quipped: 'It's about time we were owed some money from you for a change!'"

Back in 1985 the European tour, with British power-trio Tank in tow, ran from Rouen on November 16 to London on December 20, where ex-Gillan guitarist Bernie Torme's new self-titled outfit swelled the ranks to a three-band bill at the Lyceum Ballroom. As ever, word of high-spirited japes filtered their way back from the tour, including the time Brummie sound engineer 'Big' Mick Hughes gaffa-taped a cucumber and two oranges to Hetfield's mike-stand to

shooting the hitch-hiker in the head whilst, apparently, reciting the words to 'No Remorse' from 'Kill 'Em All': 'War without end/No remorse, no repent/We don't care what it meant/Another day, another death/Another sorrow, another breath...'

As Metallica began the New Year by embarking on another US tour the controversy surrounding the tragedy regurgitated the tired old issue of demonic rock lyrics, a sore point with Ozzy Osbourne, AC/DC, Iron Maiden and Judas Priest among others, but unlike the ridiculously unfair hounding of Ozzy in particular, Metallica seemed to escape quite lightly from the whole ugly affair. By the time the tour reached Corpus Christi, the offender had been convicted of first degree murder and sentenced to life imprisonment, and while he once again began shouting the words to 'No Remorse' in court while the judge was sentencing him, most observers agreed he was simply a dangerously drug-deranged delinquent destined for self-destruction regardless of his obvious love for Metallica.

"Although many of our lyrics deal with violence and death," James Hetfield explained carefully, "we don't try to promote it. Coincidentally, a song on our second album, 'Ride The Lightning', deals with Capital Punishment, so maybe they'll send him to prison with the lyrics to that to teach him a lesson."

Once the controversy had died down, Metallica could concentrate on enjoying the rest of the tour with management stablemates Armored Saint in peace. It was a well-suited pairing, socially and musically, and those who caught a number of shows on the tour reported back from

before James Hetfield sealed the performance by completing a memorable 360-degree plummet into the audience.

"I don't think we've ever toured with a band that we've gotten on so well with as Armored Saint," said Lars. "Our crew gets on with their crew and we travel in each other's tour bus. We have the same management, too. We treat them like brothers."

The Armored Saint tour also saw the birth of the 'Edna Express', as the Metallica tour bus became christened after those friendly females with loose morales and even looser underwear. A sticker on the front windscreen read: 'Don't Laugh Mister, Your Daughter's Probably Inside!', and even though neither the band nor their

according to Hetfield, "We'd spent hours and hours in the bar and then we decided to booze it up with Armored Saint, so we went up to (bass player) Joey Vera's room and drank all his beer. We were all getting really ripped and started throwing bottles out of the window - they were smashing and it sounded really neat. But that soon got so boring I threw Joey's leather jacket out and it landed in the pool... so we went down to get it and on the way back up to the tenth floor I decided to open the elevator doors between levels... we got stuck for half an hour and everyone was freaking. We finally get up to the tenth floor and by now I'm pretty pissed (mad), so I see this fire extinguisher hanging on the wall and I kinda took it down and started

...the 'Edna Express', as the Metallica tour bus became christened after those friendly females with loose morales and even looser underwear.

the front that both bands were sharing the honours equally. At the State University in San Diego on March 9, for example, honours undoubtedly went to Armored Saint who whipped the crowd into such a fervour that the front crash-barrier collapsed and caused a 30-minute delay before Metallica's set. Yet the following night at the Hollywood Palladium when Armored Saint themselves took a turn to headline, Metallica stormed through their set with an irresistible sense of revenge

sordid crew could claim to bear even a passing resemblance to the Adonis, the 'Edna' count was claimed to have been particularly generous, with some of those encountered reputedly having 'interesting' ways of opening bottles of Heineken.

Furthermore, sharing tour buses, hotels and Ednas with a like-minded rabble such as Armored Saint threw up (significant choice of phrase) an abundance of opportunities for anecdote-friendly antics. For instance there was the time when,

squirting people with it... It was five in the morning and somehow I managed to set the fire alarm off. People were fleeing from their rooms with just robes on and their kids were screaming and running around pulling each other's hair out. I went, 'Oh no!' and hid in my room... And then I heard screaming sirens, so I looked out of my window and saw two giant fire engines and police cars. People were getting into their cars and were driving away with their luggage falling out the back - and we're like sitting in our room saying, 'Fuck, what have we done here?'"

The band - who liked to be known as Alcoholica - found their drinking bouts became more prolonged when W.A.S.P. joined the tour, or more to the point when W.A.S.P. guitarist Chris Holmes joined the tour, but somehow all managed to survive the rest of the ride, whereupon Metallica flew to England to prepare for the sixth Monsters Of Rock Festival at Castle Donington in Leicestershire, on August 17. Suddenly, the cosy comfort of Stateside club gigs seemed a million miles away as Metallica were thrust before 50,000 hardened British punters on a bill which could hardly have been more unsuitable; ZZ Top, Marillion, Bon Jovi, Ratt and Magnum, none of whom could be classed as particularly heavy bands - more radio-friendly than radio-active - so how would this wicked whirlwind of megawatts fare in the middle of an afternoon of mild melodic pleasantries?

confirmed their appeal to be broader based than many originally thought. Not only that, but the band took particular delight in appearing above their old LA rivals Ratt, who by this point had become a platinum act in America.

"When we walked onstage at Donington," Lars explained, " I thought we were showing both the other bands and the

bands that end up getting compared to us. What you see is what you get, no faking."

As for the band's reception: "British audiences are strange," Lars commented later, "but once you've convinced yourselves that just because you're being bombarded with two-litre bottles full of piss, mud and ham sandwiches doesn't mean that they don't like you, and you've

TOP: BACKSTAGE AT DONINGTON, 1985;
BELOW, CLIFF, ON STAGE AT DONINGTON, SEARCHES IN VAIN FOR ANOTHER PEAR.

learnt to play your instrument while ducking and running away from things, then it's good fun."

The best example of how to deal with low-flying missiles was given that day by the unflappable Cliff Burton. Having ducked beneath a flying pear which ended up embedding itself in his bass bin, Burton coolly sauntered over to his stack, picked up the pear, took two bites out of it and hurled it back in the crowd!

A fortnight after Donington the band flew back to San Francisco to appear at a 'Day On The Green' festival, headlined by Scorpions and also featuring Ratt, Y&T, Yngwie Malmsteen's Rising Force and Victory (again, none of whom could be pigeonholed with Metallica, illustrating how the band had transcended the Thrash genre and left all their rivals behind), and then it was back to Europe again to record their third album, once more at Sweet Silence in Copenhagen with Flemming Rasmussen, the philosophy clearly being 'Never change a successful formula'.

"James and I did go to LA on an exploratory trip to try and find that one studio that said 'Metallica' on the door," Lars explained, "but it wasn't to be found anywhere. You see the studios in LA are

In the final analysis Donington did more to free Metallica from the shackles of the preconceived notion that they were simply a Thrash band than any other concert they'd undertaken thus far. True they stood out like pneumatic drills in a library, but the fact that they presented themselves so nakedly and went down so well in front of probably the most varied audience Donington has ever attracted

kids in the audience that we have a different way of presenting ourselves, way, way apart from people's preconceived ideas of what a band like Metallica is all about. And I think a lot of people are starting to understand and appreciate that what we do, and the way we do it, is real. There are none of those ridiculous pretensions in this band that seem to exist almost everywhere else with so many of the very business-like places where you get all these hit bands coming in to record singles all the time, and for us to work for a long period of time in one of those sort of corporate atmospheres just wouldn't be happening."

Work on the eight songs which became known collectively as 'Master Of Puppets' continued in earnest from September until December 26, when the band flew back to San Francisco to honour a New Year's Eve commitment. A warm-up gig with Armored Saint and Y&T was squeezed in three days later to rid the band of any rust that may have set in after months of recording booth boredom ("We came to play 'Seek And Destroy' - a song we've played thousands of times," said Lars, "and we actually had to stop half-way through the intro because we didn't know what was going on!"), and then it was New Year's Eve party time with guests Exodus, Metal Church and, interestingly enough, Dave Mustaine's Megadeth, that particular hatchet having been buried long before now. It seemed an appropriate way to end a busy but productive year, and signified to some the end of an era in a way, the end of Metallica as a fun band who didn't take themselves too seriously. The New Year would not only bring a new album but also an apparent change of attitude to the camp, intentional or not, for with the weight of big business now welling up behind them Metallica were now teetering on the edge of the Big Time.

'Master Of Puppets' did that cause no harm. Somewhat predictably it was received by those who now saw the Metallica bandwagon as the only way to travel as something of a mini-masterpiece, taking the high-decibel distortion of earlier on to slightly more even terrain. The band were edging ever closer to the Metal mainstream and critics considered it the final nail in the coffin of Metallica's Thrash connotations, an opinion the band readily accepted.

"I don't think that the word 'Thrash' ever applied to us anyway," said Lars, somewhat surprisingly since he had previously acknowledged that 'Kill 'Em All' was one of the most influential Thrash albums ever released. "Sure, we were the originators of the style because of the speed, energy and obnoxiousness in our songs, but we always looked beyond such limitations and were better defined as an American outfit with European attitudes to Metal.

"Quite honestly, I'm rather fed up with the mentalities shown by so many Thrash acts; all they wanna do is play faster and faster. What does that prove? Anyone can concentrate on speed for its own sake, but this doesn't allow any room for subtlety, dexterity or growth. Metallica is always seeking to improve, which is why we are getting attention now.

"On 'Ride The Lightning' we learnt that you could still be powerful even if the pace was slowed right down, and now we've understood that you can still hit hard even when there's subtlety in the music.

"We're right into using changes of mood and are trying to broaden out our musical base, and I think this comes across really well on the new record, where we allow ourselves considerable breathing space and opportunity to go in any direction we choose. This, in some ways, is down to the amount of time and money available for the recording of 'Master Of Puppets'. It was the first record where our (American) label, Elektra, got directly involved, and the budget therefore was vastly increased. And when there are less restrictions on you in the studio and you're not in a situation of having to rush things because your finances have run out, then you can relax and experiment a lot more."

Indeed, having more time to fine tune the album meant that even something as comparatively minor as the 'right' snare sound could be dwelt upon to the pernickety drummer's heart's content. Producer Rasmussen spent three days of careful acoustic adjustments trying to please the diminutive Dane at Sweet Sound Studios before Peter Mensch suggested flying out Def Leppard drummer Rick Allen's 1979 Black Beauty snare drum

TOP: LARS WITH SLASH AND AXL ROSE OF GUNS N'ROSES AND DAVE MUSTAINE AT DONINGTON.

(reputedly worth a cool $2-3,000) which, a week or so and several thousand dollars later, meant Ulrich could sleep peacefully at night knowing that beneath the avalanche of ear-rotting guitars his snare sound was... just... right.

Sound problems of a more serious nature cropped up when fans buying 'Master Of Puppets' whacked it on their home hi-fis and found the quality somewhat lacking. After receiving letters of complaint, MFN looked into the matter and found the cause to be the unusually long running time of the album - over 50 minutes in total - which meant the 33rpm grooves of the normal 12-inch record had been pressed too close together to achieve optimum sound quality. MFN's response was to re-release the LP (in Europe only - although it sold extremely well in the US as an import - the following February) as a

I don't think that the word 'Thrash' ever applied to us anyway. Sure, we were the originators of the style because of the speed, energy and obnoxiousness in our songs, but we always looked beyond such limitations and were better defined as an American outfit with European attitudes to Metal.

double-album on a wider-grooved 45rpm format, thereby offering the first 10,000 UK takers of the strictly limited edition package the chance to hear the likes of 'Welcome Home (Sanitarium)', 'The Thing That Should Not Be' and 'Leper Messiah' much clearer than before. For the price of £6.49 fans also got a free poster with the new, directly metal-mastered 'MOP', although the decision to simply reproduce the album's original artwork in a gatefold format disappointed some collectors.

The original release of 'Master Of Puppets' on March 7, 1986, effectively severed Metallica's last remaining ties with their days as an indie band. Their contract with Music For Nations was up once the album was out and Q-Prime, anxious to keep everything on a big league, highly corporate scale, had no intention whatsoever of renewing it.

"Actually there was a change of attitude about Metallica right from when Mensch took over," says Gem Howard, "a complete change in our relationship with the band. Mensch had worked with the Leber-Krebs management team (who'd managed Aerosmith, Ted Nugent and others in the Seventies) and he'd gone on to handle bands like AC/DC and Def Leppard, so he was a rich and powerful man who always thought on grand scales.

"On the one hand that was good for us because it meant we didn't have to pay any hotels bills when the band came to London, as they'd just stay in Mensch's huge £600,000 house in Earl's Court. But on the other hand, in the eyes of Mensch and Cliff Burnstein, Music For Nations was just a tin-pot indie label who'd never be able to do the band any good whatsoever. The fact that we'd got them three gold albums in the UK was totally irrelevant - we'd never get them to platinum status, that's what they thought.

"Really I suppose Mensch thought he'd proved his point when 'Metallica' went straight to number one in the charts, but then I reckon we could've done the same given time. After all, we put Steve Vai in the charts at number eight, and that was a bloody instrumental album! If the vibe is there with any artist you can achieve high positions in the charts, but Mensch and Burnstein didn't understand the indie scene in the UK because they just judged it by the indie scene in America, where

independent labels are for those bands who can't get major label deals. In the UK the indie market is a breeding ground for talent, and as such is totally essential to the music scene.

"So Mensch and Burnstein looked down on Music For Nations, and that translated into weird vibes from the band, because they were being told that they wouldn't go anywhere if they stayed with us. As soon as they started to believe that, our working relationship was over."

By this time Mensch had been negotiating with Phonogram for a new album deal for Metallica. Despite everything Music For Nations were still keen to hang on to what had become their most lucrative clients and they embarked on a plucky auction with their wealthier rivals. But the bottom line was that Mensch already had a working relationship with Phonogram through Def Leppard, and this was always going to decide the issue.

"Originally Phonogram offered £350,000 for the next Metallica album," says Gem, "so we went back and offered £500,000. After that Mensch went back to Phonogram and they offered him £750,000, so we just said, 'OK, bye'. Being an indie label we work on the premise of returns - we offer an amount of money that we feel we'll be able to recoup - and we didn't think we'd be able to recoup a £750,000 advance on that album. To have gone back with an offer of £1,000,000 or more would have put quite a strain on our finances at that

> In a way I think Metallica would've liked to have stayed with Music For Nations. I think the indie route gave them street cred and they loved that whole scene - the music, the people, the vibe, etc.

particular point in our career - bearing in mind that at this time the company was still quite young - and so we had to be realistic and bowed out. If we'd have put that kind of money into one act we would've jeopardised all the other acts we had, and that wouldn't have been fair.

"In a way I think Metallica would've liked to have stayed with Music For Nations. I think the indie route gave them street cred and they loved that whole scene - the music, the people, the vibe, etc. Going to a major label purely for the money meant a sell-out, a loss of street cred, and I don't think they felt comfortable with that.

Although maybe they felt a bit more comfortable with it every time they looked at their bank statements!

"At the end of the day though," Gem adds, "I think Mensch would've gone with Phonogram however much money we'd have offered. He had a sway with Phonogram because they had Def Leppard, and obviously he could say to Phonogram, 'Look, screw with Metallica and you could have problems with the next Def Leppard album', which of course meant a lot of money for Phonogram.

"The funny thing was, the first time I met Mensch after Metallica had left Music For Nations was at the Holiday Inn in Paris, and the conversation we had was incredibly satisfying for me. It went something like this:

"'Hi Peter!'

"'Oh... hi. What are you doing here?'

"'I'm doing a gig with one of our acts'.

"'Really... well, I'm here with Def Leppard. We nearly sold out our gig last night, you know'.

"'Yeah? Well our gig tonight is sold out already'.

"'Eh? Who on earth are you here with?'

"'Frank Zappa'.

"'What?! Frank Zappa? You're kidding me!'

"He was absolutely gobsmacked and I loved it. Frank Zappa is such an institution in the States, such a legend, that me telling Mensch (who was a huge fan) he was with Music For Nations was like a real blow. We actually had an act which meant more to the history of music than anything he had, and that was almost too much for him to take. He just said, 'Er... look, I'll speak to you later', and walked off, totally gutted!"

Later, when Music For Nations were about to lose the rights to the first three Metallica albums, they approached Mensch with a view to extending their contract to licence them, offering £300,000 for another five-year deal. But in his haste to bring Metallica to Phonogram, Mensch had already sold the rights to 'Kill 'Em All', 'Ride The Lightning' and 'Master Of Puppets' to them as part of the deal for future Metallica albums, and thereby lost a chance to make even more money.

Yet Mensch and Burnstein had Metallica where they wanted them and could now plot ahead safe in the knowledge that every piece in their meticulously planned jigsaw was in place.

The band for their part were doing their job: 'Master Of Puppets', which had been remixed for America by Michael Wagener, had been widely acclaimed as their most mature work to date (although once again hardcore fans complained of selling out by adopting a less Thrashier approach), and in turn had gone gold in both Britain (where it entered the charts at number 41) and America, where it made the Top Thirty comfortably.

So now it was down to Q-Prime to pull some strings and get the band as much exposure as possible while 'Master Of Puppets' was still hot. The result: the landing of the support slot on Ozzy Osbourne's mammoth March-to-August American tour, a coup of inestimable proportions for a band in Metallica's position.

"We couldn't have a better support slot than this one," Lars exclaimed several dates into the tour. "Ozzy attracts a really extreme crowd and as we are the most extreme of the up-and-coming Heavy Metal bands we are therefore getting the opportunity of playing (for 55 minutes each night) to exactly the right audience."

The Ozzy tour (dubbed the 'Damage Inc.' tour) lurched into action on March 27 at the Kansas Coliseum in Wichita and sprawled exhaustively across the American continent, chewing up all the Civic Centers, Coliseums, War Memorials and County Arenas known to mankind and spitting out the bones like pips. Aside from the good commercial sense it made it also set the seal on another lifetime ambition for the band, working with The Voice Of Black Sabbath, one of the Metal Age's founder members. The only sour note occurred when Metallica's innocent gesture of soundchecking with Sabbath songs - in the hope that the Great Oz would wander onstage and jam with them - backfired when Ozzy thought his support band was taking the piss and, seething with indignation, confronted Lars over the matter.

Nearly three months into the tour there was controversy of a more sinister nature when at Long Beach Arena in LA a fan fell from the balcony and died from horrific head injuries. With their time-honoured talent for never checking their facts properly and jumping to conclusions based on inaccurate assumptions that suit their headline-writer's points of view, certain tabloids screamed about how 'wild man of rock' Ozzy Osbourne had been involved in the death of another innocent young kid, predictably leading the anti-Metal do-gooders on another crusade of parental outrage. What they failed to mention, strangely enough, was that the incident occurred during Metallica's set. Ozzy was sipping tea backstage at the time and wasn't even informed of the tragedy until the following morning - and that no-one was to blame other than the kid himself, who it seems was hardly in a fit state to be balancing on the edge of the balcony in the first place.

After a short break in which Metallica flew to Scandinavia to appear at the Saapasjalka Festival in Wvaskyla in Finland and the Roskilde Festival in Copenhagen

We couldn't have a better support slot than this one. Ozzy attracts a really extreme crowd and as we are the most extreme of the up-and-coming Heavy Metal bands we are therefore getting the opportunity of playing to exactly the right audience.

(the unlikely bill for which also featured Phil Collins, Elvis Costello and Big Country), the US tour continued on July 11 at Green Bay, Wisconsin, and meandered south to a climax at Hampton, Virginia, on August 3. In the meantime, on July 26, Hetfield had broken his wrist after fooling around on a skateboard shortly before a show at the Mesker Theater in Evansville, Indiana, and for some of the final Ozzy shows the audience was treated to the rare sight of guitar roadie John Marshall stepping from the wings in true understudy fashion to fill in on rhythm guitar, while James struggled manfully in front of the mike stand with his arm in plaster.

Mishaps aside it had been the band's most successful undertaking to date, effectively breaking the back of America and returning sales figures of over 500,000 for 'Master Of Puppets' by the end of it. By and large Glam trends still prevailed in the US, with the likes of Mötley Crüe, Ratt and Bon Jovi hogging the front covers and FM airwaves, but with Flagship Metallica in the ascendancy and the likes of Anthrax, Slayer and Megadeth sailing in their slipstream, the heavier end of the Metal market was beginning to be taken very seriously indeed.

August was spent kicking back after the exertions of the Ozzy tour. James and Cliff formed a fun band back home in Frisco called The Spastic Children. Lars flew to Europe to hang out with old friends in Copenhagen and London, creating a legend one particular evening when, on leaving the St. Moritz club in London's Soho, he stumbled drunkenly into a taxi in the early hours and responded to the driver's "Where to, guv?" inquiry by replying with a slur, "Denmark, please".

By September 10 the band - with John Marshall (now the guitarist with Metal Church) still filling in for the well-plastered Hetfield on rhythm guitar - were back on the boards again, kicking off a European tour at St. David's Hall in Cardiff and, with old mates Anthrax in support, calling at Bradford, Edinburgh, Dublin, Belfast, Manchester, Sheffield, Newcastle, Birmingham (where Diamond Head's Brian Tatler turned up for the encore of 'Am I Evil?') and London. Reviews in the UK Metal press frothed with hysterical hyperbole about this pairing being the best true Metal package to scour the country in ages, and the noises emanating from within both camps seemed to reflect the general feeling of a boys-only high school beano.

Ironically, within a week the tour would be remembered with heavy hearts. The Hammersmith Odeon show on

September 21 would turn out to be the last UK show by Metallica in their present form, and as such the shattering end of a carefree era.

"After the gig at Hammersmith," Scott Ian recalled later, "there was a party back at Metallica's hotel. Cliff and I went on a little tour of the off-limits places in the establishment. We raided the kitchen and just messed about. I think there might have been a fire-extinguisher or two involved as well. At the end of the party, Cliff, James, Kirk, Charlie (Benante, Anthrax's drummer), Frankie (Bello, Anthrax's bassist) and I made a pact that...

JAMES WITH BANDAGED WRIST DURING THE 'PUPPETS' TOUR.

...we would come out together onstage at the approaching Aardschok Festival and do some songs in our underwear. Well, we never got to that Aardschok show..."

Stories suggest that the driver of the
bus might have been drunk at the
time of the crash; that the window
next to the bunk on which Cliff was
sleeping was illegally unprotected
by bars; that Cliff, for some spookily
unknown reason, had swapped
bunks with James just before the
accident occurred, and so on.

CHAPTER FOUR

THE ULTIMATE LOSS

Of Puppets' tour had finished I waited until the band had left the country for Europe and then slipped away for a few weeks' holiday in Cornwall," recalls Gem Howard. "We were all so pleased with the way the tour had gone and particularly with how Metallica were fast becoming one of the most talked-about bands around. We'd all worked so hard for so long and suddenly, before our very eyes, everything was beginning to pay off, the band was on the crest of a wave and the future couldn't have looked brighter.

"Then I picked up a copy of *Sounds* one Wednesday morning, opened it up and nearly fell over. It was stunning, really. Incredibly shocking…"

LEFT: CLIFF ON STAGE DURING ONE OF HIS LAST APPEARANCES WITH METALLICA ON THE EARLY PART OF THE 'MASTER OF PUPPETS' TOUR IN 1986.

Metallica were soon back in business and making all the inevitable 'Cliff would've wanted it this way' noises.

Howard's words perfectly encapsulate the tragedy of the events of Saturday September 27, 1986. Fresh from their triumphant UK tour Metallica had headed once more for Scandinavia where they'd played three shows at the Olympen in Lund, the Skedsmohallen in Oslo and at the Sonahallen in Stockholm. While travelling overnight to the fourth, the Saga in Lars' hometown of Copenhagen, their tour bus skidded on an icy road near the small Danish town of Ljungby and crashed into a ditch. Most of the entourage received minor injuries. Cliff Burton, just 24, was killed instantly.

As with most incidents of this nature, the exact sequence of events remains blurred by rumour and conjecture. A cloud of mystery still hangs eerily over the whole episode. Stories emanating from various sources of fluctuating reliability suggest that the driver of the bus might have been drunk at the time of the crash; that the window next to the bunk on which Cliff was sleeping was illegally unprotected by bars; that Cliff, for some spookily unknown reason, had swapped bunks with James just before the accident occurred, and so on.

In reality, the cold facts are these: Cliff was asleep in one of the eight bunks on the coach when, just before 5.15am BST, the coach careered out of control, causing him to be thrown through the window next to where he was lying. He was then crushed by the vehicle landing on top of him in the ditch. He hadn't stood a chance.

Of the rest of the band, Lars had broken a toe and both James and Kirk were left with bruising. Tour manager Bobby Schneider suffered a dislocated shoulder and another member of the road crew was concussed.

Danish police arriving at the scene of

the crash immediately arrested the driver as a matter of routine, but later released him without charging him after further investigation revealed that the cause of the crash was black ice on a particularly nasty bend in the road. The whole episode was simply a cruel, tragic accident.

The gap left by Burton's death yawned across the pages of tributes run by the music press the week after the tragedy. In *Kerrang!*, for example, advertisements were taken by friends and fans alike; a bleak, black double-page spread ran messages from the Zazulas ('The Ultimate Musician, The Ultimate Headbanger, The Ultimate Loss, A Friend Forever') and Anthrax ('Bell Bottoms Rule!! Laugh It Up, We Miss You'), while Music For Nations also took out a page ad which simply read: 'Cliff Burton 1962 - 1986'. The pain ran deep.

"The band very nearly called it a day when Cliff died," says Gem Howard. "Their instant reaction was: 'There's no point in going on', because the unit was broken, the chemistry was ruined. Whoever they brought in would change the band, because if you've got four elements joined together you've got a certain thing, but if you change just one of those elements you've got something completely different. It's like the difference between H20 and H2S04: one (water) you can drink, the other (sulphuric acid) will kill you - and all because one element of that chemical formula has been changed. As far as Metallica were concerned, breaking their formula could've been disastrous."

In the end they decided to carry on, as most bands do when faced with a choice between splitting with their honour intact or picking up with a replacement member from where they left off and continuing to rake in the money. Unlike Led Zeppelin, Metallica were soon back in business and making all the inevitable 'Cliff would've

wanted it this way' noises. After burying their great friend in San Francisco they wasted no time in searching for a successor, pressed all the way by Mensch and Burnstein who, true to hard-nosed management form, had already begun rescheduling the remainder of the tour which Cliff's untimely demise had interrupted.

It is a somewhat macabre coincidence but Mensch and Burnstein are not inexperienced when it comes to handling rock tragedies. Singer Bon Scott died when they managed AC/DC and Def Leppard's Steve Clark died more recently, not to mention the horrific Rick Allen incident, when the Def Leppard drummer lost an arm in a car crash. Both bands, guided by Q-Prime, went on to earn greater financial rewards.

But back to Metallica: one story surfacing around this time had Megadeth's Dave Ellefson offering his services, at least as a temporary replacement, a move which provoked Dave Mustaine into threatening all manner of retribution if his sidekick was pinched. Another story, since verified by Metal Blade's Brian Slagel and MFN's Gem Howard, claimed that Armored Saint's Joey Vera had been approached to join the band, but like John Bush before him had refused to leave his own band in the lurch by running off in search of a safe buck.

In the event the official announcement made at the end of October by Elektra A&R man Michael Alago, speaking at the annual CMJ Seminar in New York City, revealed that the job had in fact been given to a little-known youngster and big Metallifan called Jason Newsted, who'd previously been struggling through the swampy Thrash Metal backwaters with Phoenix-based Flotsam And Jetsam. Newsted had, in fact, been more than just

RIGHT AND OPPOSITE PAGE: JASON NEWSTED, CLIFF'S REPLACEMENT.

I heard about the job
through some friends
and I didn't sleep for
a week practising.
Jason Newsted.

the bassist of the band; he also doubled up as chief songwriter, spokesman, booking agent and manager, but he clearly felt that the chance to leap-frog over his indie label contemporaries into an altogether more lucrative commercial league with Metallica was an opportunity not to be squandered.

"I heard about the job through some friends and I didn't sleep for a week practising," he enthused at the time, and while some might rebuke such a brazenly mercenary attitude, others contend it was the most sensible option for an unknown in his position to take.

Newsted's background certainly didn't cut him out to be a rock star. Growing up on a Michigan horse farm in a close-knit family, his first love was quite naturally horses, and by his teens he was helping his father show Arabian steeds on the Great

Lakes State's circuit. Yet influences from two older brothers, who'd developed interests in sport and music (mainly Seventies funk like Earth Wind & Fire and The Ohio Players), soon had him looking further afield for his kicks.

"Then one day in junior high, somebody brought in the first Kiss album," Jason explained, "and that pretty much changed everything for me."

For some strange reason, he wanted to be Gene Simmons. On his fourteenth birthday he asked his parents for a bass guitar, and for the next four years practised as hard as he could, playing along to Geezer Butler on Black Sabbath records and Geddy Lee on Rush albums. Before long he'd begun to cut his teeth on local garage bands, eventually taking the plunge and heading for the plastic promises of Hollywood with little more than his bass,

amp and $300 to his name. Only he ran out of money by the time he'd reached the town of Phoenix, deep in the punishing Arizona desert, and ended up having to claw his financial situation back on to an even keel by working as a sandwich slinger and dishwasher in local eateries.

After five months in Phoenix, Newsted was befriended by a like-minded local, a drummer called Kelly David-Smith, and between them they formed a self-proclaimed Power Metal outfit called Flotsam And Jetsam, along with vocalist Eric A.K. and guitarists Edward Carlson and Michael Gilbert (who completed the line-up in February 1985). By August they were turning heads with a demo they called 'Metal Shock', a track from which ('I Live, You Die') was chosen by Metal Blade's Brian Slagel to appear on the 'Metal Massacre VII' album. Later in the year the band's second demo, '1985 Bootleg', was raided by New Renaissance Records, selecting 'Hammerhead' and 'Iron Tears' for their own 'Speed Metal Hell II' compilation.

For the rest of 1985 Flotsam And Jetsam supported just about any Metal band who passed through the South West of America: Alcatrazz, Armored Saint, Malice, Megadeth, Autograph and many more. Sufficiently impressed with their progress Slagel put up the money for a full album, and by the summer of 1986 had delivered 'Doomsday For The Deceiver', a highly-rated début which inspired some commentators to suggest the band might be destined for the same league as Metallica.

"I'm glad bands like Metallica and Slayer have been signed to major labels," Newsted told co-author Putterford, ironically in a special issue of *Kerrang!* which also featured a Cliff Burton tribute poster, "because that has opened a lot of doors for the whole new wave of Metal that's around right now. I don't know if Thrash will ever reach a point where you'll hear it being played on the radio as much as Genesis or anything like that, but at the moment it seems to be picking up popularity and that's a good thing..."

Little did he know that just days after

that interview he himself would be part of the band who were breaking down the barriers...

After a series of rehearsals in America, Newsted (alias Newkid) was to make his début with Metallica in Japan, where the band were in turn making their début, at Shibuya Kokaido in Tokyo on Saturday November 15. On arrival in Japan the newcomer was upset to have been left out of the traditional gift-giving custom, whereupon fans lavish piles of presents on their heroes, as he was mistaken for a member of the road crew.

"So he had a temper tantrum," said Lars. "Poor guy, maybe we should have got him a T-shirt with the statement: 'I'm Jason, Dammit. Gimme A Gift!'"

After the first gig, however, Lars took time out to admit to the press that Newsted had settled into the band quickly: "Being onstage with Jason felt really good from the start and he's fitting in well. I just wish that he'd relax a bit more at photo sessions. Every time he poses he looks like someone from Anthrax!"

As for the inevitably touchy subject of playing without Cliff for the first time: "I got over the shock of Cliff's death some time back," Lars commented. "Obviously we regret him not being with us, but we're sure his spirit is never far from the band."

Two days after the first show in Tokyo, Metallica headed for Nagoya on the bullet train, where they played for the second time with Jason at the Kinro Kaikan. Then it was to the Osaka Festival Hall (where Deep Purple recorded most of 'Made In Japan', a fact which had Lars kissing the side of the stage where Ritchie Blackmore stood on August 15 & 16, 1972), and a show on Kirk's birthday (November 17) which is best remembered by those in attendance for the way Lars ruined the middle of the set by playing completely out of time. Later that evening, worse for wear after their usual encounter with Absolut vodka, Lars and Kirk trashed the hotel bar toilet, claiming they were doing it in honour of Cliff's memory.

"I woke up with a pile of puke to my left, a pile of puke to my right, all the lights on and still fully dressed," moaned Kirk. "I couldn't find my room key, then I realised it was in the puke. When I checked out the receptionist asked for the key, and I did a runner!"

The short Japanese tour ended with two shows at the Sun Plaza Hall in Tokyo on November 18 and 19, and then it was back to America where a brief spurt of

dates with Metal Church had been rearranged from the summer. This was to be the true test for Jason Newsted, in the heart of the band's homeland where Cliff was probably the most popular member of Metallica, but the reviews gained from the last handful of shows in 1986 generally proffered the proverbial thumbs-up.

"All hail the Kings Of The New Age Of Metal!" raved one rag. "No doubt this was the year of Metallica. No band in recent memory have had such extreme twists of fortune in one year while at the same time capturing the hearts and minds of a loyal following that has multiplied into a vast, planet-wide legion of fans... Metallica have never stopped gaining speed and momentum, their forward thrust only slightly slowed by the shadow of death itself..."

For some observers, though, Metallica just wasn't the same without Cliff; he was the essence of what the band was originally intended to be, the free spirit, the clown, the fun element. In many ways he was the most precious reminder of life before Big Business became a necessary evil, before the innocent fun-filled cult became a big ugly bulldozing bandwagon.

Yet others pointed to a growing maturity and musical sophistication within the band and suggested that in the cold light of day Cliff's passing might be seen as a water-shed of sorts, a catalytic spark amid a tricky transitional stage, and something which allowed Metallica to progress more freely. The injection of new blood certainly seemed to give them a tighter edge, as well as the kick it needed to jolt them into a new dimension. Cruel as it sounds, some saw the end of Cliff as the beginning of the rest of Metallica's career.

First there were still some loose ends to tie. After Christmas they flew to Europe to complete dates which had been affected by cancellations the previous Autumn, starting on January 8 with a show in Copenhagen which naturally held an enormous amount of emotional significance, and then stalking across the Continent to a conclusion at the Aardschok Festival in Zwolle, Holland, this time with a supporting cast of Scrap Metal (actually a joke warm-up band comprised of members of Metallica's road crew playing covers!), Laaz Rockit, Celtic Frost, Crimson Glory, Metal Church and Anthrax. Reports back from the event (remembered by and large as a sweat and urine-swamped nightmare of Crimean War proportions) claimed Celtic Frost and particularly

> **For some observers, though, Metallica just wasn't the same without Cliff; he was the essence of what the band was originally intended to be, the free spirit, the clown, the fun element.**

Anthrax were the bands of the day, but the headliners were given the benefit of the doubt by those who pointed accusing fingers at the iffy acoustics of the smelly old aircraft hangar, and indeed at the length of the bill, which meant that most fans had been standing in the most appalling conditions for the best part of nine hours before Metallica took to the stage for their 90-minute grind.

The set for this first European foray with the new line-up remained essentially the same as the one which saw the band through the 'Master Of Puppets' (aka 'Damage Inc.') tour the previous year - albeit enhanced by a more impressive visual presentation afforded by a new lighting design. 'Battery', 'Sanitarium', 'Whiplash', 'The Thing That Should Not Be', 'Seek And Destroy', 'Creeping Death', 'Fade To Black' and the 'Am I Evil?'/'Damage Inc.' segue remained the backbone of the show, only for Aardschok there were the added distractions of Newsted's bass solo (a definite no-no in most critics' eyes, especially with memories of Cliff Burton still too warm to prevent comparisons) and a free-for-all finale of 'Blitzkrieg', which had every member of Anthrax, Metal Church and Laaz Rockit, plus a couple of Crimson Glories, conspiring between them to degenerate proceedings into a marauding mess.

With all outstanding commitments sewn up, the band returned to their San Francisco base at the end of February for a few weeks off before writing for the next album was due to begin in March. Lars claimed at the time that the band were laden with new riffs and themes knocked up into rough ideas at soundchecks and rehearsals during the last tour, and that after such a long time on the road they were itching to return to the studio. However, work became hindered after they moved into an expensive Marin County rehearsal studio and found the plush surroundings weren't conducive to what they were trying to achieve, so for a while activities took place outside the compound, a bizarre scenario which ended in Hetfield once again breaking his arm in a skateboarding accident, this time as he miserably fluffed a manoeuvre in an empty swimming pool.

Fortunately Q-Prime were only just completing the move from Music For Nations to Phonogram (via their subsidiary label Vertigo) in Europe, so the band had time on their side and didn't need to rush

the recording of their next album. Indeed, as Phonogram assumed control and a whole new team of people took hold of the reins, a new strategy was suggested which would effectively keep the fourth album on hold for another year.

PolyGram, the parent company of Phonogram and Polydor among others, had in fact taken control of the forthcoming Monsters Of Rock tour, headlined by Phonogram artists Bon Jovi in Britain and Polydor's Deep Purple elsewhere in Europe, and it made sense that Europe's most prestigious Metal tour should be used to promote the company's newest and most prestigious signing. The only snag as far as Q-Prime could see was that Metallica wouldn't have any new product ready to flog on the tour, so the idea of an EP of cover versions was hatched, a gap-bridging exercise of classic proportions, which Metallica set to work on in Lars' newly soundproofed garage during July.

If the whole concept behind the 'The $5.98 EP - Garage Days Re-visited' was just a tad calculated then it certainly didn't deter the punters. Released by Phonogram in August, it broke into both the US and UK Top 30s (actually hitting number 20 in the UK), flaunting praise a-plenty for its grisly interpretations of obscure rock artifacts. Yet those of a more objective persuasion could be forgiven for viewing the move, despite the emphasis on the crafty '$5.98...' bit, as a deliberate cash-in crossed with a desperate attempt to preserve the band's essential street cred.

Tracks covered were 'Helpless' by Diamond Head, 'The Small Hours' by Scottish band Holocaust, 'Crash Course In Brain Surgery' by Welsh power-trio Budgie, a medley of 'The Last Caress' and 'Green Hell' by cult US hardcore band The Misfits and 'The Wait' by Killing Joke - although the latter was left off the EP in the UK, thereby keeping the record to four-tracks in order to qualify as a single and stand as a candidate for inclusion in the national singles chart.

The original idea was to record a clutch of NWOBHM tunes, something Lars in particular had been hammering on about for some time, but according to the

irrestrainably verbose drummer: "When we came to rehearse a few of the songs we had in mind, to be honest they just didn't sound right - we

We were drinking and drinking and just got a little fucked up, and Lars was, like, leaning on the sound desk spilling his drink all over the place and telling the sound man to give it 'more kick drum, more kick drum'.

This, like, really pissed the Purple sound man off, so he just grabbed hold of Lars and said 'Off you go!' It was hilarious... Lars was like a human jellyfish as he hit the seats.

weren't getting into them. So we widened the net a little and came up with some stuff going even further back, and a couple of things that are a little more recent."

The story went that all five tracks were recorded in four days and mixed in a

further two. Lars took the trouble to str in the press that the record was purely of fun after the slog of the Ozzy tour, a collectors' item for the hardcore fans w were probably frustrated that new mat from the band wouldn't be available fo some time. But couldn't it also be rega as a cheaply-made throwaway designe purely to wring a few extra bob out the band's current high profile?

Another publicity stunt thinly disgu as an innocent gesture of goodwill tow the average fan-in-the-street came on August 20 when, after weeks of expert teased speculation, Metallica played a 'secret' warm-up gig for Donington at t miniscule 100 Club in London's Oxford Street, under the somewhat transparar pseudonym of Damage Inc. Those fans possessing even the most modest of IQ having sussed out the scam from the s actually began queueing outside the ve at 8.00am, causing police to be ca by 9.00am in order to move them along. However, within a couple hours hundre of fans blocke the street and the club was forced to s selling tickets four hours early in an att to quell the increasing unrest. The publicity people purred with satisfaction.

The show its was pure bedlam diabolical condit the inescapable heat and dangerous la of oxygen eventually causing Jason Newsted to faint on his UK stage débu temporary replacement was a rather bemused Brian Tatler. As a 'warm-up' the band, the conditions were certainly appropriate, although in reality no band could claim to have rehearsed sufficier for a huge outdoor show in front of 65, people by struggling through their pac a shoulder-to-shoulder sweatbox.

Two nights later came the real thin Castle Donington. On the first ever all-American Monsters Of Rock bill Metallica were positioned third in a line which also featured Bon Jovi, Dio, Anth W.A.S.P. and Cinderella, perfectly plac to make life extremely difficult for labelmates Dio and possibly even to st the thunder from under the powdered noses of the girlie-orientated Bon Jovi.

Donington was also to be the band first official UK appearance with Jason

Newsted, an added attraction which had many backstage pundits betting on a triumphant return for Metallica to the festival at which they'd made such an impression. But as the day unfolded somehow the event fell flat, suffering from a poor PA sound, the lack of any kind of light show and perhaps a lack of preparation.

The band simply put in a poor performance, leaving some observers to point out that when it came down to it, none of the four members were particularly good musicians at all. Jason, sorely lacking the personality of Cliff Burton, didn't appear to have fully settled into the band, and his playing occasionally seemed hesitant. The two guitarists also had moments when their dexterity came under question. And Lars, noted for his inability to keep a steady beat at the best of times, often seemed more interested in posing for photos by ever-present on-stage photographer Ross Halfin than in doing his job.

To their credit, they later admitted that Donington had been pretty disastrous for them the second time around. "We just didn't pull it off," said Lars, "don't ask me why." And in their defence it should be remembered that Donington is a notorious minefield for support bands who're seen as even the slightest threat to the headliners, and that most bands except those topping the bill traditionally encounter all manner of mysterious, niggling 'technical' problems on the day. On this particular occasion helicopters circling distractingly low over the festival site during Metallica's set, emblazoned with the Bon Jovi logo (although the band weren't in fact in them), hardly helped matters either...

Just over a week later, on August 29, the Monsters tour reached Nuremburg in West Germany, where once again Metallica lined-up third on a bill, this time headlined by Deep Purple and including Dio, Ratt, Cinderella, Helloween and Pretty Maids. A boozy encounter with the band the previous evening at their hotel found

METALLICA, CIRCA 1986, LEFT TO RIGHT: JAMES HETFIELD, LARS ULRICH, KIRK HAMMETT AND JASON NEWSTED.

them keen to wash the Donington performance out of their hair. "We were shit," Lars told co-author Putterford, while band photographer and mascot Ross Halfin danced half-naked on a table in the bar. "We can't wait to get out there and put things right." All the signs pointed to this being a much better event than the UK version.

Metallica were, in fact, a much fitter proposition this time, more groomed than gruesome, more studied than staggered. Even Deep Purple bassist Roger Glover hauled himself onto the side of the stage to watch the set, which pleased the band no end: appearing on the same bill as Deep Purple was something the band couldn't even contemplate in their wildest dreams just two or three years earlier. Indeed, backstage, Lars spent most of the day trying to persuade Ross Halfin to introduce him to Purple drummer Ian Paice, so that he might get the chance to have his picture taken with his hero. Despite their own elevated status and increasing claims that they'd begun to get carried away with their success, there still seemed to be something of the excited fan in the members of Metallica.

Just two summers before, Lars and James had shown what Purple fanatics they were when, during a break in the Armored Saint tour, they flew up to St. Louis to catch one of the legendary group's reunion shows. Drunk by the time they got to the venue, however, the evening very

nearly ended up with the two of them sporting their own shades of deep purple... in bruises.

"We got our passes and they let us watch the show from the mixing desk," Hetfield recalled. "We were drinking and drinking and just got a little fucked up, and Lars was, like, leaning on the sound desk spilling his drink all over the place and telling the sound man to give it 'more kick drum, more kick drum'. This, like, really pissed the Purple sound man off, so he just grabbed hold of Lars and said 'Off you go!' It was hilarious... Lars was like a human jellyfish as he hit the seats.

"Then, towards the end of the set, they're playing all their old heavy numbers like 'Smoke On The Water' and 'Speed King' and we were all well fucked up by now. Lars was passing out on my shoulder, we were like thrashing around a couple of rows. Some people got mad, and this one guy got all his friends - and these guys were on drugs or something - and they were obviously looking for trouble. Lars had crashed on the floor somewhere, I'd lost him. Anyway, this guy threw his girlfriend into me and said, 'Watch it, man!' He clobbered me in the face and his friend jumped up from behind. I was pretty beat up, I had a black eye for two weeks on the tour..."

Two years on Metallica were very much pinching themselves at the thought of sharing a stage with Purple. The night after Nuremburg the show moved over to Pforzheim, where the line-up remained the same with the exception of Pretty Maids' withdrawal, and Metallica once again acquitted themselves the way they wanted to with the likes of Ritchie Blackmore in the vicinity.

"Not bad for a snotty little Thrash band from San Francisco, huh?" Kirk quipped as he trotted down the ramp at the back of the stage with the cheers of 30,000 Germans soaring through the late afternoon summer breeze. And who could disagree?

"Not bad for a snotty little Thrash band from

... AND JUSTICE IS DONE!

JASON NEWSTED

KIRK HAMMETT

JAMES HETFIELD

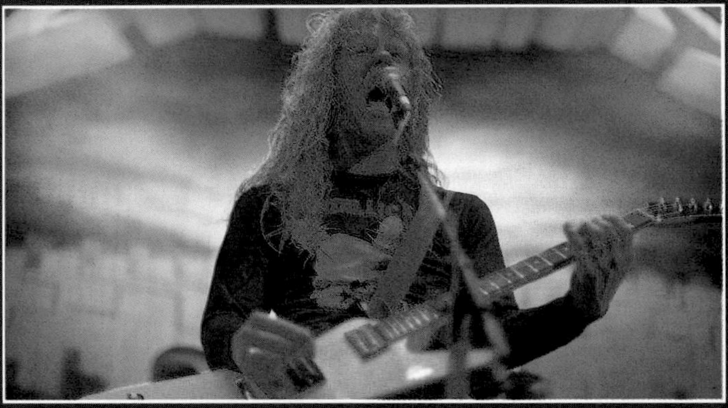

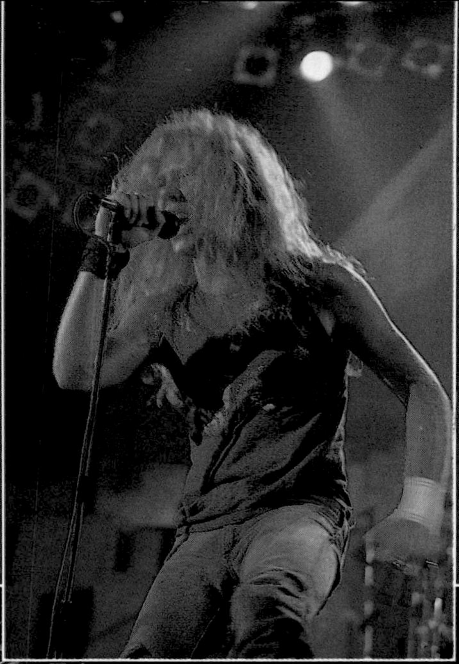

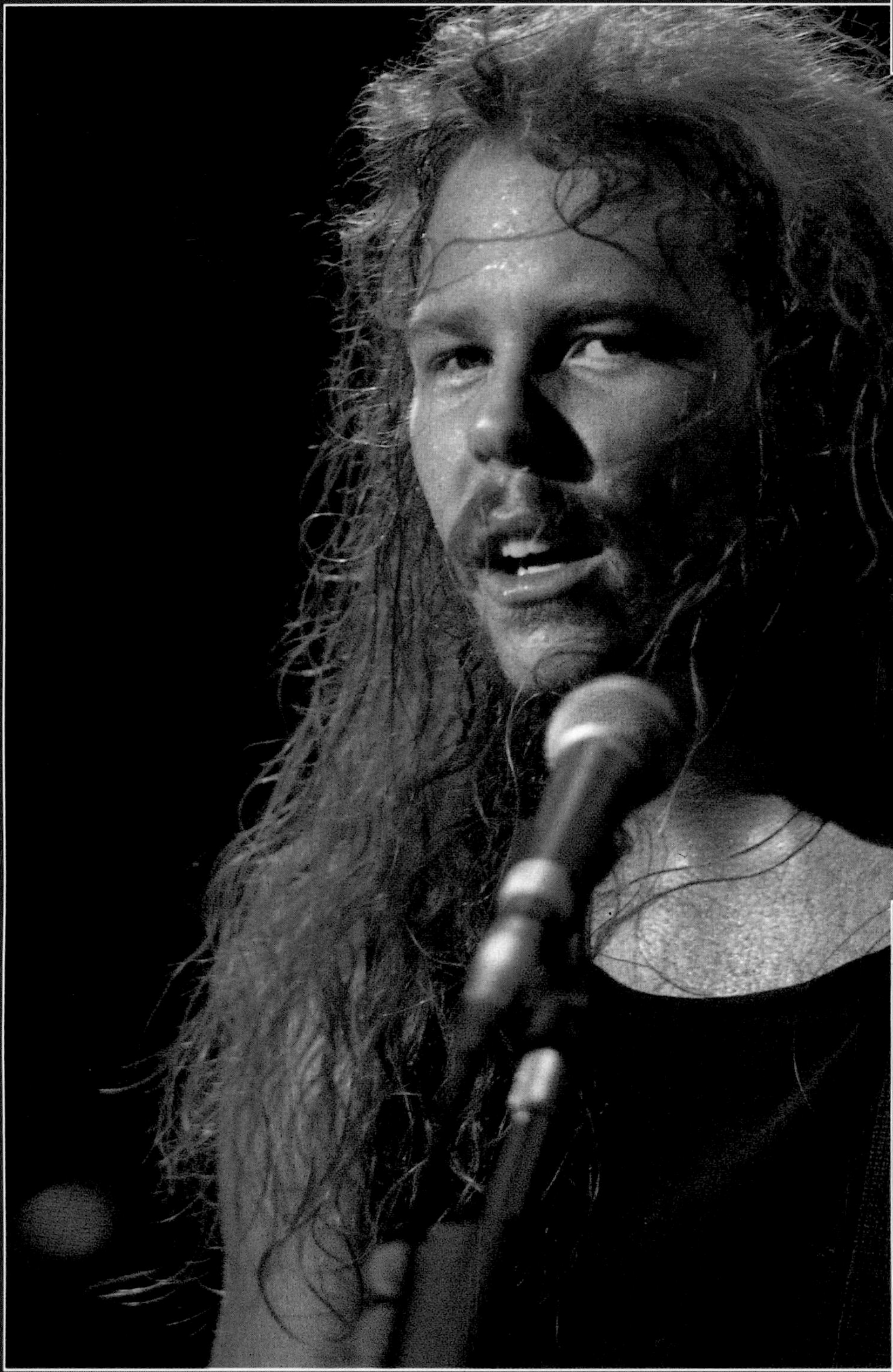

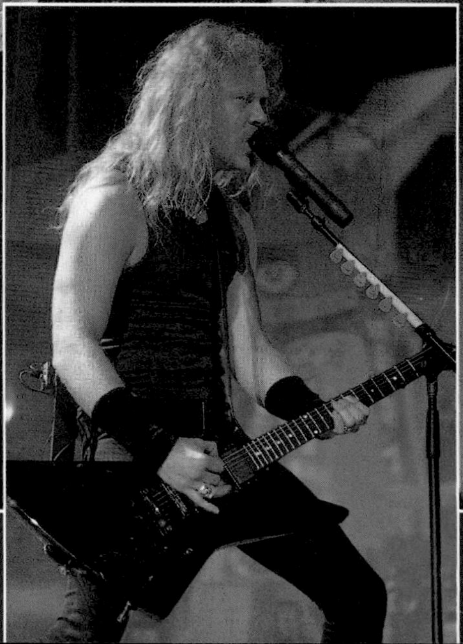

Back in the States after the Monsters
tour Metallica could finally turn their
thoughts to a new album, their first
with Jason Newsted, who'd now
been with the band for almost a
year. Most of November and the first
fortnight of December was spent
writing new material - a process
which typically meant swapping
around bits of riffs until a song
started to take shape within - and by
mid-December they had committed
nine fresh tracks to tape in demo
form, one more than was usually
taken into a recording studio.

CHAPTER FIVE

ROUGH JUSTICE

DORIS.

It's about the court systems in the US where it seems like no-one is even concerned with finding out the truth any more.
Lars Ulrich

Another foreign factor in the new recording process was the introduction of producer Mike Clink whose work on the multi-platinum Guns n'Roses album 'Appetite For Destruction' had made him the most talked-about knob-twiddler of the moment. After just a month of work on the album at One On One Studios in LA, though, Clink had given way to the tried and trusted Flemming Rasmussen, and rumours abounded concerning the reasons behind the sudden switch.

"The whole business was purely down to availability," Lars explained in an attempt to play the situation down. "We had nine songs ready to go by mid-December, but we found out that Flemming wasn't going to be available until something like the third week of January. We had a choice to make - whether to get going or whether to wait for Flemming, and we thought that seeing as we always need about a month in the studio simply to get

our confidence up and to get the basic sounds together, we might as well start that part of the job without Flemming.

"We'd heard lots of good things about Mike from Guns n' Roses and we knew that he was available so we just got in touch and asked if he'd be interested in helping out for the time that Flemming was unavailable. There was never any doubt that Flemming would eventually come in on the project, so Mike was really brilliant in being prepared to help out just in the early stages.

"The thing with Metallica is that we are a very different band to record than anyone else and we really can't do without Flemming. Mike understood this and he was really 'happening' in putting a lot of work in without really getting much credit for it."

Nevertheless it wasn't until Rasmussen joined the party at One On One studios at the end of January that the new album started to take shape. By April Lars could reveal to the press that the title of the record was '... And Justice For All' - cynically chosen to represent the general theme of injustice - and a couple of

months later as the finishing touches were being carefully made, the inexhaustible drummer offered his own analysis of the tracks therein.

'Blackened': "This song is a bit different from all our other opening tracks in that we've purposely avoided the whole over-long, half-hour, huge build-up intro bullshit thing which we've done for a couple of albums now and everyone else seems to be doing it as well. So this song comes out blasting at you from the word 'go'.

"Musically it's a bit different from what one would consider to be a typical Metallica opening track, because it takes a couple of sharp turns later on in the song and becomes almost like a full-circle type of thing. It just sort of goes from one extreme to another, and then back again.

"Lyrically, this one's about old Mother Earth and how she's not doing too well nowadays. It's just about all the shit that's going on in the world right now, and how the whole environment that we're living in is slowly deteriorating into a shithole. This is not meant to be a huge environmental statement (?) or anything like that - it's just a harsh look at what's going on around us."

'...And Justice For All': "This one is something like ten minutes long. It also goes through some different shit along the way, with various feels and a lot of changes. It's pretty uppety-tempo for the most part, but it's a little different for us in that the main riff

is centred around this weird drum beat that I came up with in the rehearsal studio one day.

"It's about the court systems in the US where it seems like no-one is even concerned with finding out the truth any more. It's becoming more and more like a one-lawyer-versus-another-type situation, where the best lawyer can alter justice in any way he wants."

'Harvester Of Sorrow': "Compared to some of the other stuff on the album it's a bit more basic and instant. It's a real heavy, bouncy, groovy type of thing. Plus, it's not too long by Metallica standards - it's only about five-and-a-half minutes long.

"Lyrically, this song is about someone who leads a very normal nine-to-five type life, has a wife and three kids, and all of a sudden, one day, he just snaps and starts killing the people around him."

'The Shortest Straw': "It deals with the whole blacklisting thing that took place in the '50s, where anyone whose view was a little out of the ordinary was immediately labelled as a potential threat to society. There were all these people in Hollywood whose views didn't fit in with the mainstream, and they were all shoved out of the entertainment industry because of their beliefs."

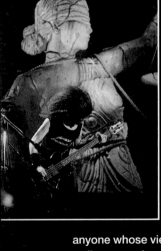

'To Live Is To Die': "This is our 'obligatory' instrumental... compared to our previous instrumentals, 'The Call Of Ktulu' and 'Orion', this one's a lot huger and more majestic sounding. It's also a lot looser in some ways

in that it's a bit more of a jam-type thing and not quite as square...

"A lot of people might give us flak about this one because it features some stuff written by Cliff a few months before he was killed, but the truth of the matter is these riffs were just so huge and so Metallica-sounding that we had to use them. We're certainly not trying to dwell on Cliff's death or anything like that - we're simply using the best ideas we had available, and this was one of them."

'Eye Of The Beholder': "The lyrics to this one are pretty much self-explanatory. It's basically about people interfering with your way of thought, and really how America is really maybe not as free as people think."

'Frayed Ends Of Sanity': "It's a bit more musical and intricate than most of the other songs on the album. It's got a pretty long musical middle part with a lot of changes and some pretty cool melodies. Overall, it's pretty much a mid-paced sort of thing, but it's really intricate and it might take a couple of listens before you can get into it.

"Lyrically, it's really just about paranoia - you know, being afraid, but not really knowing what you're afraid of."

'One': "This was something that started out being about having no arms or legs, being deaf and blind, just like being a brain and nothing else. It's kinda scarey and very fascinating all at once. Anyway, James had these ideas for lyrics and then Burnstein suggested a book to me called called 'Johnny's Got A Gun' by a man called Dalton Trumbo, which is about this guy who comes back from the war like that, so James got some input from that."

'Dyer's Eve': "It's basically about this kid who's been hidden from the real world by his parents the whole time he was growing up, and now that he's in the real world he can't cope with it and is contemplating suicide. It's basically a letter from this kid to his parents, asking them why they didn't expose him to the real world... It's a really heavy subject, and our management is sure that trouble is on the way. But we like it, so..."

...So that was that.

In the midst of all the talk about the new Metallica album, however, the band took time out to reflect on the past. 'The $19.98 Home Vid - Cliff 'Em All', a cobbled-together, bootleg-style video tribute to their late colleague was released first in the States (in early December), where in no time it had shifted some 90,000 copies, and later (April) due to popular demand in Europe. Fittingly for a band who'd previously ignored all the pressures

of the MTV age and refused to spend time and money on glossy promo videos, it was a low-budget, warts'n'all, fans-eye affair, like a personal scrapbook with moving pictures, which offered a revealing insight into what life in the band was really like between 1983 and 1986.

"We didn't want that typical glitzy Bon Jovi crap," stressed Lars, "and the only reason that it ever came out was because we happened to be looking through our private video collection and just thought it'd be fun to let the fans see some of the shit we had."

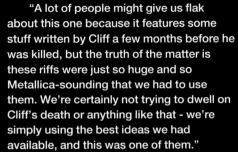

As with the 'Garage Days' EP it was tempting to view the 'Cliff 'Em All' video as another low-cost/big returns way of raking in a few hundred thousand extra bucks, but equally it was hard not to actually believe the band this time when they protested their innocence from any rip-off scam. Perhaps this, despite the 15 quid a throw snag, really was just a well-meaning exercise in nostalgia.

"It is a kind of tribute," said Lars, "but it's done Metallica-style. We could have sat for hours talking on and on about what a brilliant bass player Cliff was, what a wonderful person he was, but that wouldn't have been the whole reality of it. It would've turned out very sombre, but we wanted to see him remembered in a happy kinda way.

"In a curious way we had to make fun of him as well in order to do that. We didn't go, 'Cliff was born in such and such a place and he grew up with flowers in his hair...' We talked about Cliff's pot-smoking and how he was always late for everything, because in that way we remember him for what he was, and we remember him with real emotion and love.

"The still photos that we used and the home footage show Cliff's personality in its truest light. If people are upset by that (some fans had written to the band complaining about the shots showing Cliff smoking dope) then it's only because they're afraid of the truth. Like it or hate it, be it good, bad or ugly, it's certainly honest.

"And to be honest, I don't think the quality of the footage is going to affect us adversely. It's not as if this video is going to act as an introduction to Metallica to a kid in Stoke or Derby. It won't be the first time he's seen us so he'll know what the score is. He might well find some of the shit amusing though, like seeing James in 1983 on the Metallica/Raven 'Kill 'Em All For One' tour wearing a pair of spandex trousers!"

Also in evidence was footage from Cliff's second ever gig with Metallica at The Stone in San Francisco on March 19, 1983, some shots from the 'Day On The Green' festival in August 1985 and the Roskilde Festival in July 1986,

some stuff from the Ozzy tour the same year and a chaotic collage of off stage tomfoolery right from the very bottom of the band's closet.

"When I look at the video... it tends to make me think of the good times," explained Lars, "times when we were goofing around. But there are about three minutes at the end of the video where there are a bunch of still photos of Cliff shown with the bass harmony part of 'Orion' playing in the background. That part is definitely a lot more serious and I do get a bit emotional when I see it. That was the piece of music that we played at Cliff's funeral so that was the only way we could end the video. I know that's the way Cliff would have wanted it."

Quite what all the publicity about Cliff Burton was doing to the confidence of Jason Newsted, however, was uncertain. All Lars could say was: "We haven't really talked about the video with Jason very much... he's not really said too much about it. I'm not actually sure I want to get into this, but basically however Jason feels about the video is how he feels. What I do know is that Jason has always had a lot of respect for Cliff, both as a bass player and as a human being, and you can't ask for more than that."

Newsted, meanwhile, was anxious to get '...And Justice For All' out and finally establish himself as a 'full' member of the band. Yet work on the record was once again interrupted by the chance to indulge in a quick burst of big pay-days, when Q-Prime landed their boys a spot on the

first American Monsters Of Rock tour, starting on May 28 and headlined by Van Halen with Scorpions, Dokken and Kingdom Come also in tow.

By and large, however, the tour was a commercial flop, reflecting in part both the new Sammy Hagar-fronted Van Halen's lack of popularity, and the general downturn in concert ticket-sales all over America during the summer of 1988. On the whole attendances were disappointing, but as accountants scuttled nervously around juggling figures as best they could for promoters who were clearly getting their purse-strings burnt, Metallica were sneaking out the back door with arguably the most favourable profile of all the bands on the bill. At the Tampa Stadium gig in Florida, Sammy Hagar even pulled Lars and Kirk to one side before they went on to ask, with a mixture of sarcasm and concern: "What's all this I hear about you guys stealing the show every night?"

"Well, I mean I don't want to brag about it," Lars bragged, "but usually the best way of metering what's going on is T-shirt sales, and after the official Van Halen/Monsters Of Rock event shirt, we've outsold everyone else in T-shirts on every show we've done so far on this tour. Which is an amazing thing in itself, but it's not like something that's gone to our heads, or that we've started living by, it's just a simple fact of life on this tour. The most brilliant thing of all about it is that we're doing our thing with no holds barred and people seem to be taking to it. That's what blows me away, really."

The business side of the band had really become Lars' domain by this point, for while James just blundered through each day with his bottle of Absolut and the other two kept very much in the background - Kirk with his comics, Jason with his Walkman - it was the busybody drummer who buried himself in the group's financial affairs, hassling the management with endless phone calls and fax messages and wanting to learn all the time.

He had a fascination for aspects of the band's career like merchandise sales, training a jealous eye on the way bands like Iron Maiden made mega-bucks from T-shirt sales in the States, and he was always looking to follow suit. Whether it fitted in with the image he liked to present to the press or not, Lars was very much obsessed with making money, and working with the likes of Mensch and Burnstein he soon developed an astute business acumen. An almost photographic memory also meant

he could store facts and figures in his mind for extremely long periods of time, an ability which gave him the means to bore a drinking partner to death when talk got around to ticket sales or balance sheets.

During the summer of 1988, as the Monsters tour limped across America, Lars and James took the opportunity whenever there was a break in the schedule to fly up to Bearsville in upstate New York to oversee the mixing of the new album. The plan was to complete work on the project by the time the tour hit Detroit on June 18, and then finally have it in the shops shortly after the end of the Monsters tour, on August 1.

The mixing was being looked after by Steve Thompson and Michael Barbiero who, like Mike Clink, had established themselves as hot property after working on 'Appetite For Destruction', a choice which some saw as yet another concession to fashion by a band who masqueraded as anti-establishment heroes. Yet Lars refuted such suggestions vehemently. Perhaps he was just a little embarrassed that more perceptive observers could sense the band's decisions were now being made almost entirely by the corporate-minded Q-Prime.

"We used Thompson and Barbiero because they mix a band according to the band," Lars snorted defiantly. "They don't have their own set ways, and James and I just knew what we wanted. If you just take a look at their track record you can see that they work with a wide range of artists from Dokken to Madonna to Guns n' Roses..."

Preceded by the single 'Harvester Of Sorrow' (backed by yet more covers, this time Budgie's 'Breadfan' and Diamond Head's 'The Prince', leftovers from the Mike Clink period - a package which reached number 20 in the UK charts), the double '...And Justice For All' album finally saw the light of day on September 8. The long delay - it came almost two-and-a-half years after 'Master Of Puppets' - worked a

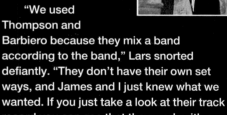

treat in building up expectancy to fever pitch and it entered the UK charts on September 17 and reached number four.

With a somewhat boring degree of inevitability the Metal comics seized upon it like The Holy Grail itself, lavishing superlatives in its general direction with crazed abandon. But yet again, as it marked another step towards maturity, another shuffle into the mainstream and perhaps a first, tentative surrender to the magnetism of commerciality, fans from the early days received it with scornful disdain. Some simply didn't like it at all.

"I couldn't help but think it was pretty awful," says Gem Howard, "and that's not sour grapes. I mean, the drum sound was terrible - like someone banging on a couple of cardboard boxes. And I think a lot of the material on the album was really just 'filler' stuff. In my mind it wasn't a patch on 'Master Of Puppets', which was really cohesive as a complete work, with every single track being incredibly strong. Like 'Ride The Lightning', which had a very meandering Side Two, '...And Justice For All' seemed to me to be overlong (in fact a tortuous 65 minutes long) and over-ambitious."

Even James Hetfield later admitted the production in particular was lacking: "I think we went for something we didn't really achieve. We wanted a really up-front, in-your-face album and it didn't really work out. The drums are awful, there's no depth to it."

To add to the criticism about the drum sound some observers also commented on the lack of bass on the album, while others complained bitterly about the acoustic - yes, acoustic! - guitar on 'To Live Is To Die'. Even more shockingly, certain friends of the band overheard Lars confessing that Kirk Hammett hadn't played on the album at all, surmising from that that there was something of a guitar power-struggle going on between Hetfield and Hammett, and that the more dominant figure of Hetfield was insisting on his own way in that department with increasing stubbornness.

From the very outset '... Justice...' seemed to be dogged by a mess of back-biting, a situation the band undoubtedly brought upon themselves. Those with half-decent memories, for example, picked up on the cover design, which craftily echoed an idea originally used on Samson's 1981 album, 'Shock

LARS IN FREE-BOOTING MOOD DURING A METALLICA FIXTURE AGAINST IRON MAIDEN.

Tactics'. While the likeness of 'One' to 'Fade To Black' from 'Ride The Lightning' didn't go unnoticed either, nor did the fact that the track occupied the slot at the end of Side One - the traditional stamping ground for the band's more balladic numbers - something which provoked accusations of contrivance.

"I agree and I'm not going to defend that," Lars admitted. "I had about 72 different running orders written on a Federal

JASON AND KIRK WITH FLEA AND ANTHONY KIEDAS OF THE RED HOT CHILLI PEPPERS.

Express envelope at my house... I lost three days sleep because I knew that people were going to pull it apart."

But in general the plaudits outweighed the poison arrows and the band could cushion the blow of jibes about them betraying their Thrash principles roots and sucking up to the Yankee dollar by wallowing in the knowledge that they were

making new friends all the time. Besides, they clearly felt they could twist the issue with counter-claims that what they were really doing was breaking down the barriers for others of a similar disposition.

"If we're doing anything at all," Lars was at pains to point out, "we're showing all the doubting Thomases up there on the 22nd floor of record companies who had ignored us for a long time. The music scene now is basically a product of what certain people in certain high-rise buildings will allow you to hear. It's been like that through the Seventies and Eighties. When we came along we had a very different attitude to what was going on, in as much that we didn't give a shit what was going on with those people up there, we were doing what we were doing. We were the first band to have the chance to go into the masses and have that attitude about it. At the same time as we were called 'door openers', we were also showing the idiots at the record companies, the select few who get to choose what people listen to, that they aren't always right."

After blowing out the cobwebs with a warm-up show at the Troubadour club in LA billed as Frayed Ends, the 'Damaged Justice' tour began proper on Saturday, September 24, at the Edinburgh Playhouse, where British fans got the first chance to check out the band's most ambitious, not to mention most expensive, stage set to date: a decaying house of justice littered with crumbling 'stone' pillars and lions, the centrepiece of which being the statue of Blind Lady Justice featured on the album cover, a towering monolith which gets gradually built during the set by a system of wires and pulleys before being smashed to pieces during the frenzy of the title track, '...And Justice For All'.

From Scotland the tour (with support from Danzig) ran through Wales (Newport), Eire (Dublin) and Northern Ireland (Belfast), before heading gradually south to London and finishing with a third night at Hammersmith Odeon on Tuesday October 11. The two-and-a-half-hour-plus set included five tracks from the new album, as well as a snippet of 'To Live Is To Die' which followed Jason Newsted's bass solo, and climaxed some nights with a punishing eight-song encore section, occasionally including a surprise blast of Iron Maiden's 'Prowler'.

After the UK, Europe; after Europe, America... the 'Damaged Justice' juggernaut gaining momentum with every change of direction. Indeed, a new twist to the forward thrust of Metallica's bid for megabuck Nirvana came as the band finished 1988 with a clutch of sell-out dates at Long Beach Arena in LA: for the first time in their entire existence Metallica succumbed to record company and management pressure and humbly joined the MTV Club by filming a promo video for their next single.

The rather dubious honour of début promo was to be bestowed upon the track 'One', which had previously stood proud at almost seven-and-a-half minutes long, but which the record company felt might be a contender for *Top Of The Pops* territory if it was pruned to a more digestible length and packaged with the traditional amount of promotional pizzaz. Stooping from a previously lofty position of almost religious abstention, Lars conceded with a token amount of reluctance, clutching at the compensation of having the original version of the song on the B-side.

"We thought about it and realised that this was a chance to expose more people to Metallica music. And by putting out a single with the edit on one side and the full version on the other, I think we've reached a situation that everyone in the band is happy with. As long as everyone knows it's an edit, that OK. And if it turns more people on to our music, and introduces them to the whole album or even our earlier records, then that's very cool."

Taking scenes and dialogue from the film of Dalton Trumbo's 1971 'Johnny's Got His Gun' novel, the video for 'One', directed by Michael Soloman, depicted the horror of a man trapped in the ultimate isolation of physical and sensory paralysis. Footage of the band performing was restricted to fashionable black and white, and Lars claimed they always retained the right to bin the whole thing if it "wasn't right". Patently it was, receiving its first airing on MTV's 'Headbangers' Ball' and thereafter slotting nicely into the expected heavy rotation groove. In response the single shot to number 35 in the US and 13 in the UK.

To complete Metallica's welcome into the establishment, America's NARAS organisation (National Academy of Recording Arts and Sciences) announced in January that it was nominating the band for a Grammy in the new Best Heavy Metal/Hard Rock Artists category. Other

nominees were AC/DC, Iggy Pop, Jane's Addiction and Jethro Tull, but as Metallica were also asked to perform 'One' live at the awards ceremony in Los Angeles - before an estimated global TV audience of over one billion - most agreed that the result was a foregone conclusion.

Except the NARAS. To boos from the audience and universal gasps of disbelief, the winners were in fact the most unlikely candidates of them all - the whimsical, now predominantly folk orientated, Jethro Tull - a decision which left Metallica squirming with embarrassment. Elektra, too, had egg on their faces: they'd already printed up thousands of 'Grammy Winners' sashes to be displayed in retail outlets all over America. The event was shown on TV in America on February 22, but the

debate about the outcome raged on for weeks afterwards.

"Yes, they played their little hearts out in front of millions on TV, clearly expecting to win," Tull's wily old frontman Ian Anderson told co-author Putterford, "and, bless their little spandex trousers, they were a bit upset at losing to us - especially as the nearest we get to Heavy Metal is playing our mandolins quite loudly! No, we certainly didn't expect to win a Grammy either.

"But the point of the Grammys is that each category is decided by the votes from 4,000 members - effectively the peer group of the creative end of the music business, like songwriters, publishers, recording engineers, musicians and so on - who send in their votes by post. It isn't decided by the public or the popular media.

"And I suppose in voting us winners they are recognising the fact that we've been around a long time and we're still refusing to go away! I mean, of course we're taking it all as a bit of light-hearted fun, because we've managed to go 20 years without winning a Grammy and I'm certain we could have gone a few more. But I'm pleased we've won it, and as for Metallica... well, they didn't win it, hard luck chaps, but I'm sure you'll live to fight another day."

"We were told by the people who run this thing that it always takes a couple of years for the Academy to focus in on what a new category is all about," said Lars, looking for a shred of comfort. "They've had all this before with strange nominees and winners in those specific fields. I think the real victory was playing live and being part of the televised telecast. The visual and audio aspects of that will stick far longer than all the 'who won or lost' business. People will remember the song, and in the end who walks off with a gold-plated gramophone really isn't important. Jethro Tull is being thought of as such a weird choice that in weeks to come it'll be seen as the time they had a chance to have a finger on their pulse but in the end stuck it up their ass.

"It is the first time that a lot of people have seen a Heavy Metal type band on a show like this and it showed those who have painted those misconceptions of HM in their minds that they were wrong. I think a lot of people probably thought there'd be satanic cross-burning and ritual sacrificing! The ignorant people in middle-class America who have these weird views saw otherwise. We also managed to represent in five minutes what the metallica thing is all about, to those who don't know, from the subdued bits to the heavy parts.

"From that point of view it was a great thing for us. Of course I'd be lying if I didn't tell you I was disappointed, human nature is that you'd rather win than lose, but Jethro Tull walking away with it makes a huge mockery of the intentions of the event."

Metallica could perhaps take comfort in the knowledge that unjust Grammy snubs are by no means uncommon. The worst example occurred in 1964, a year in which The Beatles captured America and dominated their charts as no other performers have done before or since, at one point holding down the top five places

I think a lot of people probably thought there'd be satanic cross-burning and ritual sacrificing! Lars

**The tour statistics drove the point home:
over 250 concerts played; 32,500 guest
passes used; 4,500 tins of Sapporo beer
sunk; 3,000 drum sticks smashed into
matchsticks; 1,650 sets of guitar strings
and 750 sets of bass strings burnt through;
over 30 million interviews given by Lars Ulrich.**

in the *Billboard* singles chart during the same week. That year NARAS awarded the Grammy for Best Vocal Group to MOR drudges The Anita Kerr Singers who have never reached the US Top 40 in the singles or LP charts, let alone demonstrated the tiniest fraction of the creativity shown by The Beatles. Over the years other rock legends, Presley, Dylan, The Stones, The Who, Hendrix, The Doors and Led Zeppelin among them, have been similarly ignored in favour of candidates more 'acceptable' to NARAS.

Lars and his taciturn sidekicks could also console themselves with the fact that the fortunes of 'One' took a sharp upturn after the Grammy controversy, and that the current US tour was raking in the readies at an incredible rate. The band, the previous personification of gutter-level Garage Metal, standard bearers for the underdog and the yardstick for the alternative, were now lording it up in five-star hotels, stretch limos and private planes. Like the leaders of the Punk revolution just over a decade before, who denounced materialism until they became rich themselves and mysteriously changed their tune, Metallica were now revelling in the trappings of their wealth and finding the whole palaver an increasingly awkward concept to defend.

The 'Damaged Justice' tour (with Q-Prime stablemates Queensrÿche, support act on the European leg, still opening the show) continued to trundle through the stadia of the States until May, when Metallica switched their attention to the Far East. After débuting with a solitary show in Auckland, New Zealand, they played their first shows in Australia - in Melbourne, Sydney and, after a 2,000-signature petition from local fans, in Adelaide - supported by the dangerously similar Aussie band Mortal Sin, before

heading for the sake buckets and sushi bars of Japan, where they could now comfortably fill 13,000 seater arenas.

Those fans who did make the shows were also offered the chance to legally tape the event - an idea proposed by co-manager Burnstein who, after seeing it work for the Grateful Dead in America, suggested installing a platform behind the sound-desk where something like 200 fans could, after purchasing a special ticket, wave their pocket-sized recorders in the air without fear of having their collars felt.

"I really don't think it affects anyone," Lars considered, when pressed about the possibility of these tapes being transformed into over-priced vinyl bootlegs. "I mean, you know that there's really a lot of people into this shit, and no-one's gonna tell me the people who collect bootlegs are not gonna buy the new Metallica album when it comes out on the proper label. These people are die-hard

fanatics who collect all this shit and, if anything, I think it makes the whole situation better.

"Also, if we know there's 200 kids out there taping a show, then it's gonna give us a kick in the ass because it's gonna make sure that we've got it together up there on stage. So, all in all, I think it's a fine situation to be in."

Back in the West the tour danced to the tune of the Yankee dollar throughout the summer before heading South during October for shows in Brazil and Argentina. A batch of British and European dates, which included two nights at Brixton Academy in London, had then been pencilled in for November, but after returning to the sanity of home after their groundbreaking exertions in South America, it became obvious to even the slave-drivers at Q-Prime that the band were beginning to enter the advanced stages of exhaustion, and respite was now essential.

The mighty Metallica machine finally ground to a halt at the end of 1989, drained of energy and emotion after nearly 18 back-breaking months of gruelling roadwork. For a band who once couldn't get a gig for love nor money they hadn't done badly.

The tour statistics drove the point home: over 250 concerts played; 32,500 guest passes used; 4,500 tins of Sapporo beer sunk; 3,000 drum sticks smashed into matchsticks; 1,650 sets of guitar strings and 750 sets of bass strings burnt through; over 30 million interviews given by Lars Ulrich (probably). No wonder the band claimed their heads were spinning at the end of it all.

But the carousel hadn't stopped for long, merely paused for a swift oil change before swinging into action again. Metallica, it seemed, weren't just a band regarded by some as 'the business' any more, they were now a business which just happened to be a band.

CHAPTER SIX

FOR A FEW DOLLARS MORE

We were freaking out about how quick things happened for us.

If 1990 was supposed to be a more leisurely year for Metallica, then it certainly didn't get off to a good start. No sooner had Christmas turned its back than the band were informed by Cliff Burnstein that they'd been put up to record a track for Elektra's 40th anniversary celebration album, 'Rubaiyat'... and the deadline was early January. The reluctance with which the band accepted their label's 'invitation' clearly indicated they had no say in the matter.

The idea for the album was that each of Elektra's big-name artists would record a song from the label's back catalogue, a concept which was unlikely to pose any problems for most of the label's roster who could choose from a wide selection of appropriate material, but for Metallica the options were rather more difficult.

The band's gut reaction was to go for something from Queen, but they were informed that another Elektra act had already chosen to cover a Queen song, so an alternative was quickly sought with deadline time approaching. James went through his Tom Waits albums in search of something which might be appropriate, Lars considered a track from 'Fire Down Under' by Riot, but decided it was too obvious, so rather than resort to covering a Tracy Chapman or Anita Baker standard the band went back to Elektra and pleaded with them for the chance to do Queen's 'Stone Cold Crazy'. Eventually they relented and the band threw the track down as quickly as they could before returning to the rather more agreeable task of winding down after the exertions of 'Damaged Justice'.

The first four months of the year were in fact deliberately low-key, with each member having a chance to do his own thing and get away from the ever-expanding entity that was Metallica. They were awarded with a Grammy for 'One' in February, no doubt a belated exercise in redemption after the controversy of the previous year, and despite their low profile, the band were never far from the news pages of music publications the world over.

Another noteworthy news story with a Metallica connection was the release of a double CD on the Vertigo label - 'New Wave Of British Heavy Metal '79 Revisited' - celebrating the tenth anniversary of the NWOBHM, compiled by Lars with help from *Kerrang!* editor Geoff Barton and featuring no less than 30 bands from that particular era.

All the same, Metallica wouldn't actually be seen in the flesh until the early summer. Indeed, the first batch of dates pencilled into the schedule for 1990 was a European trip in May with selected shows in Britain, Germany, France and Holland, before they lunged headlong into their fifth studio album.

This brief European spree, the band were at pains to point out, wasn't a proper tour, and as such there would be no new album to promote and no new stage show. However, Phonogram couldn't let the occasion pass without releasing something or other and a number of marketing exercises were mooted. One idea was to release 'Stone Cold Crazy' on the B-side of a single which didn't have an A-side, the

hope being that the record would hit a novelty nerve which would court extra publicity and interest. But as Elektra had yet to release the compilation for which the track was originally intended, the idea wasn't contractually feasible.

Eventually Phonogram came up with 'The Good, The Bad & The Live: The Six And A Half Year Anniversary 12" Collection', a box set of all the band's EPs to date - 'Jump In The Fire', Creeping Death', '...Garage Days...', 'Harvester Of Sorrow' and 'One' - plus three previously unavailable live recordings of 'Harvester Of Sorrow', 'One' and 'Breadfan'. It made good business sense for the record company, tempting fans to shell out for the whole caboodle just to obtain the three extra tracks, which could have been

"It sucked - I hate playing in England now because the audiences here are so lame, and tonight they hardly moved at all. It was almost like being in a graveyard! Lars.

released on a single EP in its own right. But once again Lars found himself in the embarrassing position of having to meekly justify what, at £14.00, was a rip-off exercise he clearly didn't agree with, but which for political reasons he had to go along with. (In response, the fans largely gave the offering a wide berth; it crawled into the UK charts at a lowly 56

on May 19... and sank without trace the following week).

The band were obviously a lot happier jumping up on stage again and storming through their old set with the minimum of fuss. Just three shows were lined up for Britain - Wembley Arena on May 23, Birmingham NEC on the 25 and Glasgow SECC on the 26 - plus another five festival headliners on the Continent. Although to try to counter the argument that the band were removing themselves even further from street-level by graduating to the Wembley Arenas, they also threw in a surprise slot at the Marquee on May 11, opening up completely unannounced for Metal Church and giving those who'd turned up early for the show (and spotted the tell-tale Danish flag on the drum-kit) a rather sudden shock of realisation.

The band were just about holding on to their credibility by this time, although the kind of self-congratulation now being practised on stage began to draw stiff criticism from old fans. The irritating omnipresence of photo-aholic Ulrich had definitely started to grate, to the extent that during the Wembley show, when he stepped out from behind his kit to talk to the audience, certain sections of the crowd actually booed him. Backstage after the Wembley show

Lars was clearly unhappy with how the show had gone, confiding in co-author Russell: "It sucked - I hate playing in England now because the audiences here are so lame, and tonight they hardly moved at all. It was almost like being in a graveyard! We only did the encores because we felt obliged.

"Playing Europe is a real drag for us now," he went on to say to a bemused Russell, who pointed out to the drummer that he was in fact European, and that his attitude had always been very pro-Europe. "Yeah I know," he replied with a heavy sigh. "It's sad, but that's how I feel and that's what it's come to."

Spirits were also noticeably low at the exclusive post-gig party at London's Mayfair hotel, where the band moped around like shadows of their former fun-loving selves. Hetfield, seen supping a rancid Budweiser, even conceded that he wasn't allowed to touch his favourite tipple, Absolut vodka, any more, an admission which seemed to confirm the worst fears of those who'd seen signs of Metallica becoming a boringly serious band.

They returned to exile in the States after Europe and, after a trip to Canada where they'd been offered the irresistible chance to open up for Aerosmith at two huge festivals, began knocking together ideas for the next studio album. By the autumn they'd formulated 12 new ideas, and could finally enter the One On One studios in North Hollywood on October 6, where this time they'd decided to work with producer Bob Rock who, having made his name producing the likes of Mötley Crüe and Bon Jovi - the kind of bands Metallica had always tried to distance themselves from - had to be seen as representing yet another huge leap towards the mainstream for the band.

"I've heard Bon Jovi this, Bon Jovi that," sighed Lars, "but the fact of the matter is, Bob Rock's got an incredible ear for attitude and feeling. Bob's convinced that the four of us playing together has a certain magic or vibe that never happens with me doing drums to a click-track and James coming in and overdubbing rhythm guitars. We've been proud of how musically accurate our records have been in the past and how in tune everything's been, but it's gotten so clean and antiseptic that you've got to wear gloves to put the damn thing in the CD player!

"This time around it'll probably have more of a feel of what we're after when we're playing live; a lot looser, groovier, underplayed and overplayed when I want it to be. Being incredibly precise and accurate worked for a while. I'd like to try something different for a change."

Which effectively meant the band had agreed with the criticism that '...And Justice For All' was an over-ambitious mêlée of extravagant arrangements and were determined not to repeat the same misjudgement of approach.

"'...Lightning', '...Puppets' and '...Justice...'.'," Lars told *RIP* magazine, "each one of these records was more progressive than the one before. Each one had longer songs than the one before. I think we've lost a little bit of that groove stuff that we used to do... So we said, 'Wait a minute, it's time to really shift gears. It will just be so boring and predictable to do another '...And Justice For All', with ten-minute songs and 55 time-changes'.

Metallica had in fact made a pact with the American *RIP* mag whereby each monthly issue would carry an exclusive report on the progress of the new album, right from the writing of the material to the final mixing stages. The idea, not surprisingly, had been suggested by Lars, who probably couldn't have laid down one single drum track without conducting three or four interviews about it anyway. But while it was hardly anything other than a shrewd publicity campaign in the guise of a favour to a few journalist friends - ensuring a massive, appetite-whetting build up to the launch of the album as well as ensuring favourable blanket coverage from America's biggest Metal monthly thereafter - it also illustrated how the band could now rely on almost total backing from the world's rock publications, a relationship which had become an essential cog in the Metallica machine.

Despite the growing ranks of disgruntled fans who expressed a belief that the band had completely sold out and were just a few steps away from hairspray and make-up, the world's rock press clustered around the band like quivering disciples, gasping at every twitch, fainting at every blink. Journalists fell over themselves to get in the band's good books by ejaculating praise every time the band moved a muscle, and the press departments at the band's various record companies around the world were virtually made redundant in the process.

When Metallica had started in 1982 the UK's *Kerrang!* was the only recognised Metal magazine on the scene. By the start of 1992 there was *Kerrang!*, *Raw*, *Metal Hammer*, *Rock Power*, *Metal Forces*, *Thrash'n'Burn*, *Rock Attack*, *Hot Metal*, *Riff Raff* and *Rock World* in the UK alone, while America could boast leather-bound log-books like *RIP*, *Metal Edge*, *Faces* and many more. Elsewhere in the world, countries like Japan had scintillating intellectual tomes such as *Burnn!*, *Biva Rock*, *Rockin-F*, *Music Life* and *Metal Gear*, while most European countries were swamped by their own versions of the British trend-setters. In fact everywhere you turned there was another Metal comic screaming at you with its pseudo-aggressive visuals and its pre-pubescent patter, offering a stodgy diet of Guns

n'Roses, Bon Jovi, Skid Row, Mötley Crüe, Poison and... Metallica!

In most of these publications objectivity was virtually an irrelevant consideration, especially where big American bands (and thus opportunities of trips abroad) were concerned, and whilst none of the bands could be criticised for pandering to the publicity, the state of rock literature in general had certainly taken a dive from its respectable perch of the Seventies. Metallica, or rather Lars, milked the situation for all it was worth, hence *RIP*'s rather painstaking documentation of every phaser pushed, every guitar re-strung, every vocal overdubbed... 11 solid months of what the gushing editorial team dubbed 'Metalli-watch'. How could the album fail?

In essence the new album took shape in a number of different phases: writing during the summer, pre-production rehearsals in San Francisco during the autumn, live jams in the studio during

October and November, the meticulous search for correct drum and guitar sounds, the laying down of basic tracks (Lars first, then James' rhythm guitar, a few guide vocals, Kirk's guitar, Jason's bass, Kirk's solos and vocal overdubs), then the finalising of recording followed by the long mixing haul during the spring of 1991. At a cost of several thousand dollars per day the album wasn't coming cheap (in the final analysis it was estimated to have cost over $1 million to make), but then commercial expectation was such that no expense was spared.

If the record bosses were worried that Metallica's prolonged absence from the public eye might have lessened their appeal, they need only have referred to the 1991 Grammy awards in February where the band were once again decorated, this time for their version of 'Stone Cold Crazy'. Although sceptical about the merit of winning such an award after the 1989 controversy, the band refused to attend the ceremony, with Lars later explaining how they felt almost embarrassed to receive the award.

"...If we release anything for the rest of the Nineties," he sneered, "every year we'll get a Grammy for it just because they fucked up that first year. Nobody's gonna want me to say that but that's where it's at.

"Listen man, we go into the studio in January last year and spend about 15 minutes - give or take a day, the shortest visit we've ever had in the studio, anyway - and we put down a cover version of a Queen song from 1973 for an Elektra compilation album, and it's track 11 on side three, right, and it wins a Grammy over fully-fledged albums by, like Judas Priest and Megadeth? Don't you think it's got anything to do with, 'Gee, how can we rectify how we fucked up in 1989?'"

'Metallica', as it was eventually named, was finally ready for release on August 12, almost three years after '...And Justice For All'. Like its pretty unimaginative title, the cover of the record was a plain black sleeve simply stamped with the band's logo and the outline of a snake, and while neither idea could be considered even remotely original (numerous bands have released eponymous albums late in their career, while many have used the stark black or white cover idea), Lars claimed that they'd made that decision to distance themselves from the current Metal norm.

"A lot of things in the past few years in Metal have really gotten out of hand, and we certainly threw our two cents in there. It just hit me how silly things are getting with clichés and cartoons images. Throughout most of the eighties I was like the biggest Iron Maiden fan - they had great record covers and all these clever names for their tours. I dug it, and we copped some of that early on, but we don't want to be slaves to all of that. What would happen to Iron Maiden's next record if they took Eddie off the front cover? So we said, 'Here's 65 minutes of music in its most naked form'. We've set ourselves up to be ridiculed, but if we were afraid to be ridiculed we would have played the game a whole lot differently. We threw a Metallica logo on it and it pretty much titled itself. It's a case of 'Here's the record, here's a lyric sheet, you figure it out'. You can call it anything you want: 'The Black Album', 'The Snake Album', 'Metallica Sucks'.... Actually that's one of my favourites..."

Beneath the ominous cover (which also emphasised the band's 'official' adoption of the colour black; they now dressed almost entirely in that colour) lurked Metallica's most commercial album to date, still painfully heavy but nevertheless carefully combed for accessibility. It was a much more natural-sounding album than the art-Metal orgy of '...And Justice For All', more streamlined and less tangled. As Kirk Hammett explained: "Touring behind it ('...Justice...') we realised that the general consensus was that the songs were too long. Everyone would have these long faces," he added, referring to the times he'd look into the audience during the laborious ten-minute title track, "and I'd think, 'Goddamn, they're not enjoying it as much as we are. If it wasn't for the big bang at the end of the song...'

"I can remember getting offstage one night after playing '...Justice...'," he continued, "and one of us saying, 'That's the last time we ever play that fucking song!'"

The band later conceded that their awkward leap from the two-chord thrash of 'Kill 'Em All' to the ten-time-changes-per-verse extravagance of '...Justice...' essentially boiled down to their own musical insecurity.

"We were freaking out about how quick things happened for us," said Lars. "It's not like we had five years of paying our dues on the club circuit. There we were, playing cover songs, writing our own songs, and all of a sudden, we were touring America, making a record. And we were 19 years-old, thrown in at the deep end. We felt inadequate as musicians and songwriters, and that made us go too far, around '...Puppets' and '...Justice...', in the direction of trying to prove ourselves."

The idea with the fifth album was to capture a far more basic sound, something more in tune with what Joe and Josephine Punter could instantly relate to, without having to spend six weeks scrutinising the record for all its pretentious nuances. Perhaps the most blatant manifestation of this approach was 'Enter Sandman', with its hugely catchy chorus and sensible stomping beat, altogether the most conventional track on the album and the obvious choice for a lead-single. Sure enough, after preceding the album at the end of July, '... Sandman' shot to number five in the UK charts and number 16 in the US.

Once again the new Metallica album was received with almost universal acclaim, this time even prompting coverage by 'serious' music journals like *Time* and *Rolling Stone* in America, and the high-brow daily newspaper *The Guardian* in Britain, who, laughably, chose to portray the band as intellectuals in faded black denim, veritable Jean Paul Sartres with shaven personalities! The band had now become perceived as the acceptable face of Heavy Metal, the Thinking Man's Metal Band, the yardstick by which the rest of the genre should be measured. In fact, the reality couldn't be further from the truth.

Such was publicity surrounding 'Metallica' that a lot of people thought the band had only just formed, prompting an endless stream of interviewers to enquire when work would begin on their second album. More seasoned commentators observed yet more Ennio Morricone influences, including some actual

samples of the man's music on the track 'The Unforgiven', and even suggested the album bordered on a tribute to Morricone, something Lars begrudgingly admitted later.

Eve' from '...Justice...', was moulded from the psychological turmoil of his adolescence, when he was brought up by strict Christian Science parents and let loose into the world as a confused and slightly bitter teenager. 'The Unforgiven', brushed with whispering cellos, oozed with a simmering passion that seemed beyond the growling troll from 'Kill 'Em All'. And 'Nothing Else Matters', cushioned by the strings of a 40-piece orchestra, was a love song of unashamed admission, a rare relapse into doe-eyed romanticism by a man renowned for the blood-spitting attack of a rabid pitbull. Perhaps for the first time, Hetfield had confessed to a streak of vulnerability.

"That song was just me and my guitar on the road," he explained as the post-album inquest began. "It came together somewhere in Canada, I think. I just sat in my room working on this thing. It was a personal thing. I played it for myself. But I played it for Lars, and he listened and said, 'Man, that's pretty cool'. And I thought, 'Yeah, it is'.

"People have their own interpretations of love. For some, love is sleeping with a sheep. For others, it's just being with somebody. Love to me is being able to depend on someone else, especially being on the road. You can really lose yourself out here. Then you go home and you realise, 'Yeah, here's my base - here's where I start, and here's where it ends'.

"It's not a safe song," he added. "It takes some nerve to do. We're not supposed to do something like that. Then you turn around and go, 'Well, who said we

The idea with the fifth album was to capture a far more basic sound, something more in tune with what Joe and Josephine Punter could instantly relate to, without having to spend six weeks scrutinising the record for all its pretentious nuances.

"Yeah, James has been into this type of music for years and some of the melodies are really impressive. In fact, if you came down to the studio when we record then you'd find Morricone records lying all over the place. The same with our dressing room on the road. Jason is also into this sort of stuff, so yeah, it has had an influence on us."

Lyrically, 'Metallica' provided perhaps the deepest insight yet into the clenched mind of James Hetfield, revealing traces of sensitivity and emotion previously buried well beneath his sullen and intimidating exterior. 'The God That Failed', like 'Dyer's

couldn't? We're running the show here'."

Ironically, perhaps, in the midst of Hetfield's emotional outpourings, the other three members of the band all went through divorces during the recording of the new album, inevitably due to the constantly mobile nature of the Metallica bandwagon. This, Kirk later revealed, was

an extremely painful situation which partially inspired the track 'Wherever I May Roam'.

In the general scheme of things, the decision to embrace more common lyrical themes - like love - provided Hetfield and Ulrich with an escape route from the dead-end alley they'd turned into on '...Justice...', when they simply turned on the American TV news channel CNN, had a quick look at what was going on in the world, and decided to write a song about it. Yet with the track 'Don't Tread On Me', certainly the most topical and contentious effort on the album, they managed to attract all kinds of criticism: some, in certain cases, from the very same people who praised Hetfield's horrific portrayal of the hideously maimed war veteran in 'One', fired stinging accusations of misplaced jingoism in the wake of the Gulf War.

In fact, Hetfield maintained he actually wrote the song in August 1990, before Saddam Hussein's invasion of Kuwait, and that the flag in question was not the Stars And Stripes but a banner carried by

Culpeper's Minutemen of Virginia during the revolutionary war; a flag inscribed with a coiled-snake emblem, a replica of which was hung in the studio during the recording of the album, and a reflection of which appeared on the album's mysterious cover.

For all the pseudo-intellectual bickering, the real test for 'Metallica' was how the fan-in-the-street reacted to it, although even here it was a shame that those working on the project had to further strain the band's street-cred by premièring it in particularly crass, money-making

manner. At the Hammersmith Odeon in London and at New York's Madison Square Garden in August, fans were invited on a first-come- first-served basis to a special pre-release listening party. Naturally both venues were full, and the 10,000 fans in New York were rewarded by the appearance of the band onstage after the album had run its course, lapping up the applause in true Vegas style.

As 'Metallica' loomed into view it was clear only Guns n' Roses long-awaited 'Use Your Illusion I' and '...II' albums would contest it as the biggest Metal album of the year. And its timing, even after such a long wait, was immaculate, hitting the streets the week before the band played on the Monsters Of Rock bill at Castle Donington for the third time in six years.

Actually, some observers may have been surprised to see Metallica accept a slot on the Monsters bill below headliners AC/DC, but as Lars explained it all fitted perfectly into the band's touring strategy. "We were really keen on starting our world tour in America this time, but if we were to

Crowes, Queensrÿche and Mötley Crüe completing the bill, toiled across the European Continent throughout August and September covering no less than 18 cities with 20 concerts. Donington fell on August 17, and while AC/DC inevitably won the day, Metallica (nicknamed 'Metal Alex' by the headliners, with whom they didn't enjoy a particularly harmonious relationship - something to do with a certain P. Mensch, perhaps?) more than made up for the dismal display of '87.

Behind the scenes, however, a startling and immensely disappointing reminder of how much Metallica had changed since the early days came in the minutes before the band were due on stage. Hetfield, Hammett and Newsted all mingled with the guests backstage, chatting and joking with old friends and clearly keeping their feet on the ground. Ulrich, meanwhile, remained in his dressing room until the very last moment, finally making his way to the stage draped in towels and surrounded by a small army of hulking bodyguards. No-one was allowed to talk to him or even think about approaching him, and even members of the band's road crew visibly cringed at the sight of such pointless pomp, one later admitting that Lars' ego had got well and truly out of hand.

The Monsters tour climaxed with a free show on the Tushino airfield on the outskirts of Moscow on September 28 - an especially uncomfortable event, fraught with

I never pictured in my mind what having a number one album meant, because I never thought it was possible to have a number one record with the kind of music we play. Jason

do it that way then there would be this big gap of about three months during August, September and October. That's because you've got to wait for people to pick up on the record, because the States is so big. We also didn't want to start by headlining in Europe because it's the same old story every time: we start in Europe, we don't know the new songs, the show isn't together and we don't know our ass from our head, y'know?

"Then this thing (the Monsters tour) presented itself and obviously you can imagine how long it took me to make that decision. Playing with AC/DC is like 'it' for me. We've played with Iron Maiden, Aerosmith and Deep Purple, and short of getting Led Zeppelin to re-form and Hendrix to pop by, then it's just about as far as you can get!"

The Monsters tour, with The Black

security problems and crowd unrest - before Metallica could finally return to home pastures and the task of flogging their new product to expectant fellow countrymen. No-one expected it to be a mission impossible, as news had already reached the band that the album had entered the *Billboard* charts at number one, and that it was well on the way to topping the sales figures for all the band's previous albums put together.

"I stood there in my hotel room and there was this fax that said, 'You're Number One'," said Lars, recalling the night in Budapest during the Monsters tour when he received confirmation of his band's feat from Q-Prime's New York office. "And it was like, 'Well, OK'. It was just another fax

If people come and see us and think it's arena rock crap then that's fine. It doesn't affect me, because I know what we are doing is something distinctly different from what everyone else is doing. Lars.

from the office - just numbers on a piece of paper. It's just really difficult to get excited about it, we've never really been career-conscious, we never tried to be number one. But now we're number one and it's, like, OK."

Jason Newsted, meanwhile, took the news equally casually: "I never pictured in my mind what having a number one album meant, because I never thought it was possible to have a number one record with the kind of music we play."

The US tour finally kicked into gear in the autumn, with the band unveiling their all-new stage show for the first time at Oakland Stadium in California on October 12. Taking their lead from management stablemates Def Leppard, who'd become known for performing 'in the round' (whereby a circular stage is positioned in the centre of the arena, giving fans 360 degree burns!), Metallica's presentation focused on a futuristic diamond-shaped stage which allowed for fans to be seated all around it. Twelve microphones dotted around the lip of the stage meant James could dash easily from pillar to post without being caught out of position, sometimes creating the curious sight of all three guitarists facing different directions and spread so far apart as to almost look improbable colleagues. Lars meanwhile, not wanting to be left behind in the high-tech stakes, insisted on a drum kit which also moved around the stage on tracks, once again providing an odd spectacle for those used to the wall-of-Marshalls routine.

"He wants to be in the spotlight," sighed James. "I find it a little silly..."

Perhaps the most innovative aspect of the new Metallishow was the so-called 'snakepit' area in the middle of the stage which was reserved for competition winners and other deserving Metallica fans. Squashed into an intimate enclosure which allowed a unique view of the band in action, the fans could actually feel like they were part of the show, a refreshing change from the matchstick-men-on- the-horizon situation that occurs at most multi-purpose enormo-domes in the States.

"There's room for about 120 people inside this area," Lars explained. "We have competition winners in there, and we also send out roadies to the cheaper seats to find fans who are going totally wild and being rowdy. They are on the lookout for those fans in old Metallica T-shirts and they are then escorted into the pit right below us. That way they get spat and sweated on by James! It's really a unique way to see any show, and it's great for us to see fans right up against the stage going completely mad.

"This area," Lars stressed admirably, "isn't there for music industry types to stand there with their hands folded. Peter Mensch tried to walk certain music biz people through to the area at one gig, but we were having none of it!"

Considering the complexity of the new stage set-up, it wasn't difficult to understand why no support act was considered for the American leg of the tour. Instead, audiences were warmed by the showing of a 30-minute video which did its best to outline the band's history, briefly covering everything from the Mustaine

garage days to Cliff Burton and beyond. But while most die-hard fans didn't seem to mind this new concept, some reviewers hammered it into the ground, complaining it cheated the audience of VFM and up-coming bands of the chance of the kind of invaluable 'leg-up' that Metallica once had from the likes of Ozzy Osbourne.

The Metallica entourage now consisted of 12 equipment trucks, six buses and over 60 permanent crew members. What with all the arena-show pomposity and larger-than-life theatrics, Metallica had clearly been transformed into the kind of highly-polished corporate money-machine they once existed to rebel against. They were clearly just another fat turkey on the production line, bearing no resemblance to their former selves. But, as ever, they refuted such suggestions bluntly, although it must be said in a much less convincing manner than before.

"I think a lot of people in America right now, because we have become confident with what we are doing, are saying that we are doing the same arena rock clichés that other bands are doing," admitted Lars sheepishly. "If people come and see us and think it's arena rock crap then that's fine. It doesn't affect me, because I know what we are doing is something distinctly different from what everyone else is doing. I think we have a capability to keep ourself one step away from what everyone else is doing."

And they could still point to the opinion polls for support: at the end of 1991 Metallica virtually swept the board in all of the Metal comics' readers' polls, a remarkable illustration of the extent of their reputation. Lars' bleating insistence that they were 'doing it on their own terms', upholding strict principles and fiercely retaining their integrity may have been complete and utter tosh, but those who'd been brainwashed by the round-the-clock hero-worship publicity from the Metal media were falling for it hook, line and sinker.

A mini-backlash, however, was caused by Metallica's latest concession to the video age - a serious-musicians-in-the-studio promo for the single 'Nothing Else Matters', which MTV naturally flogged to death in helping the song reach number 34 in the US and number six in the UK during May. The concept of Metallica - former doyens of the full-throttle Sod 'Em All Thrash movement and the curse of the camera-pandering pop market - going through the motions like some kind of unshaven equivalent of Spandau Ballet was

BACKSTAGE AT THE FREDDIE MERCURY TRIBUTE CONCERT AT WEMBLEY STADIUM, APRIL 1992.

just too much to stomach, and many expressed their disgust.

In the US a number of critics were giving the band's latest arena tour a rough ride too. Most complained about the pointless indulgence of the nagging solo sections: Jason's bass solo, Kirk's guitar solo, Lars' drum solo - 'The sort of standard arena crap Metallica should be avoiding, much less acquiescing to' commented one journal - and then an unforgivably irrelevant section of the show where James joins Lars on one of his two (?) onstage drum kits and proceeds to clown around for 10 minutes or so. While no-one could fault the grandiose magnificence of the state-of-the-art stage production, some concluded the band were out of their depth in other areas.

The band also attracted criticism when they flew to London on April 20 to kick off the colossal Freddie Mercury Tribute Show - the 'Concert For AIDS Awareness' - at Wembley Stadium. While the likes of Extreme and Def Leppard angled their short sets towards a celebration of what the late Freddie was about by covering Queen songs, Metallica simply thudded through dour renditions of 'Enter Sandman', 'Sad But True' and 'Nothing Else Matters', apparently missing the point of the whole day. Although the reaction they got from perhaps the most diverse crowd they'll ever play before (who'd have thought Metallica would ever

share a bill with Liza Minelli?) must've surprised those who thought they'd go down like a dose of AIDS itself.

It was a masterstroke for Q-Prime to pull though, slipping Metallica in through the back door that their main attractions Def Leppard had opened, and ensuring exposure to an estimated worldwide audience of half-a-billion. When Hetfield returned to the stage later to sing 'Stone Cold Crazy' with the remaining members of Queen (plus guest guitarist Tony Iommi from Black Sabbath) it must have automatically added a few thousand dollars to the band's next royalty cheque, as well as burning the name Metallica on to the minds of a million or more armchair viewers. This, after all, was

Metallica hobnobbing with the establishment, up there alongside Elton John, David Bowie, George Michael, Annie Lennox and Lisa Stansfield, and arguably the culmination of everything Q-Prime had worked for for six years.

No sooner had the 70,000 fans who'd turned up to pay their final respects to Freddie Mercury filed tearfully out of the stadium than the 'milk it dry' philosophy of those who handled the band's affairs produced a particularly cunning idea of how to cash-in on the event. Within days the Vertigo label pressed and released a live EP taken from the show, featuring the three songs the band had performed on the day, and some sort of new record was claimed in the bargain. All done for the benefit of the fans, obviously.

The following month news filtered over from the States that Metallica were planning to return to the UK in October and November for an arena tour that would allow them to haul over their huge American production for the first time. Before that an historic Guns n' Roses / Metallica co-headlining tour of the States (with megastars-in-waiting Faith No More opening) was planned to clean up the stadium circuit during the summer, and beyond that... who knows? The possibilities for the heaviest band in pop are endless.

CHAPTER SEVEN

OVERLOAD

Following the Freddie Mercury tribute concert at Wembley Stadium, Metallica suddenly found themselves at No.6 in the UK charts with 'Nothing Else Matters'; playing that song at Freddie's bash obviously had the desired effect. Back in America the Metalliwagon rolled across the US and Canada. Sharing the bill were renowned hell raisers Guns N'Roses, and it was well documented that there was intense rivalry between the two bands; doing fifteen rounds with Lars Ulrich and Axl Rose's egos was heavy going.

(ROSS HALFIN)

(BERNHARD KUHMSTEAD/RETNA)

but we honestly couldn't make our minds up what to put out, there was so much stuff we'd recorded that we knew the Metallicats would be into!"

As it turned out, Metallica filled a whole 'Flightcase' (a cardboard one) full of goodies: two three-hour videos (video 1 took in the Seattle show from the '... Justice' tour; video 2 had footage from San Diego on the 'Wherever We May Roam' tour) and a triple CD, lifted direct from Mexico City. Other goodies included a 72-page booklet, crammed with Ross Halfin family-style snaps, a 'Snake Pit' pass, and a 'Black Snake' (aka: Scarey Guy) stencil, all for the princely sum of £75.

Inevitably fans complained about the hefty price, but that didn't stop the initial run of 10,000 copies selling out. Despite the 'Sell Out' feel to the whole package it has to be said, 'Live, Shit! Binge And Purge' is up there with the likes of 'Kiss Alive' and Blue Oyster Cult's 'On Your Feet Or On Your Knees' as a landmark in live recordings.

After solid touring between 1991 and 1993, Metallica lay low for the first half of '94, but the lure of the dollar sign proved too irresistible, and a small 'Summer Tour' was planned, finally evolving into the 'Summer Shit US Tour' 94, which was later redubbed 'Shit Hits The Sheds US Tour'. The tour was a scaled down version of the 'Wherever We May Roam' tour. Instead of playing the usual three-hour plus extravaganzas,

On August 8 at The Olympic Stadium, Montreal, Metallica were hit with a thunderbolt – literally. A flashpot exploded near James Hetfield who was rushed to hospital with first, second and third degree burns on his left hand and first degree burns on his right arm. Once again former guitar tech and Metal Church guitarist John Marshall filled in for James, as he did for six dates on the Ozzy tour of '86, when James had a nasty skateboard accident. Ironically, on the night Hetfield was hurt GN'R vocalist W Axl Rose sparked a riot by leaving the stage after just 20 minutes of the band's performance.

1993 found Metallica road bound once more, and wherever they roamed controversy seemed to follow. A show in the far east on April 10 at The Lebak Bulus Stadium, Java, caused a riot. 2,000 Metallifans found themselves locked out, they began rioting, and more than 70 cars were destroyed in the pandemonium. But Metallica played on regardless, in fact they hadn't got a clue what was going on. Over 80 fans were injured.

There was no such trouble at the Milton Keynes Bowl on June 5, 1993, where Metallica were reunited with their idols Diamond Head; also on the bill was former Metallica guitarist Dave Mustaine's band Megadeth, along with The Almighty. It was a totally hassle free day and to be in the Snake Pit was like being in your own little Metalliworld; hell...

there was 'Nowhere Else To Roam'!

During the summer of '93, the Metalliwagon came to a crashing halt, and was put into the garage for a much needed service and rest. After the members of Metallica had recharged their batteries they were soon hard at work mixing their up-and coming live extravaganza – 'Live Shit! Binge And Purge'. As Lars Ulrich pointed out: "We were just clearing the vaults, we wanted to put out a load of live shit,

(LFI)

2-9600
Specialists

the band went more for the throat with a solid two-and-a-half hour set.

The tour kicked off at the Darien Amphitheater, Buffalo on May 30 and climaxed at The Bicentennial Park, Miami, Florida on August 21. With their wallets filled to the brim Metallica then decided to play Monopoly with their US record company, Elektra, and take them to court over their contract with the label. It would appear that Metallica had agreed a new contract with former Elektra president Bob Krasnow, but since his resignation in July, the deal had been rejected by his successors. As Lars points out: "We've been good, we haven't gone in after every album and asked for more money. The one thing we're interested in was getting our master tapes back and making sure the songs didn't end up on toothpaste

commercials!"

Needless to say Metallica got their way; with just about every major label knocking on Q. Prime's door Lars and Co. held the trump card – the Joker (Scarey Guy). Metallica remained with Elektra.

"... it was loose enough to be loose, yet retained an edge to it, we held our shit together and it kinda kicked, I'm glad we did it"

Lars Ulrich on Donington 1995

In May 1995, Metallica finally entered the Record Plant Studios in Sausalito, California, with producer Bob Rock to record the long awaited follow-up to the multi-selling 'Metallica', which has now sold close on 15 million copies world wide, nine million in America alone. Recording started okay, but Metallica

were being continuously hassled, with rumours about a possible appearance to headline Donington Monsters Of Rock. Despite continuous denials, the rumours kept on coming. Meanwhile AC/DC dropped out of the running. And Metallica kept saying "No". But at the *Kerrang!* Awards on June 20 at the Cumberland Hotel, London, Metallica had a change of heart and agreed to play Donington, albeit very much on their own terms. They would choose the support bands and they even changed the name of the show from 'Monsters Of Rock' to 'Escape From The Studio '95'. The bands specially chosen for the occasion were Therapy?, Skid Row, Slayer, Slash's Snake Pit, White Zombie, Machine Head, Warrior Soul and Corrosion Of Conformity.

(ROSS HALFIN)

By headlining Donington Metallica had also broken the record for the most appearances at the festival (four: 1985, 1987, 1991 and 1995), climbing the bill with each visit.

It was a great show and Metallica seemed very relaxed by the whole experience, it didn't rain and they even aired two new numbers from the up-and-coming 'Load' album; both songs had a laid back bluesy feel about them, and were met with a polite rather than enthusiastic response.

Backstage, Lars was definitely in an up-beat mood: "Hell, even Slayer were smiling today," beamed the Great Dane. "The whole vibe felt very relaxed; as one-off shows go it went much better than expected, considering we've been holed up in the studio since May, it was loose enough to be loose, yet retained an edge to it, we held our shit together and it kinda kicked, I'm glad we did it."

The only other live outing for the band in '95 took the Metalliwagon (with snow chains) up into the Arctic Circle to take part in the 'Molson Annual Polar Beach Party', in the small Canadian town of Tuktoyaktuk, which is 2,000 miles north of the Arctic circle. Metallica were certainly

'Trapped Under Ice'.

Back at the Record Plant in Sausalito, Metallica ploughed on with Bob Rock and in February 1996 finally finished all the basic recording; they had 14 tracks in the can. Mixing took place at the Right Track Recordings, New York, between April and March. 'Load' was finally finished and claims to be the longest single playing CD ever recorded, boasting a running time of 78 mins 59 seconds. Was it worth the wait though? Well according to *The Independent*'s Andy Gill, "Metallica are the only heavy metal band that adults can listen to without feeling their IQ diminishing" .

Kerrang!'s Phil Alexander said: "Load is the album which every release this year will be measured by. Proof indeed that Metallica have retained their ability to set the standards and raise the stakes." Other comments include: "Pretty fucking cool" (*Melody Maker*) and, somewhat curiously, "A gripping journey" (*The Daily Mail*).

Musically speaking, 'Load' is a much more mature album than 'Metallica'. There's a lot more going on musically speaking. James Hetfield's love of Southern/Country music comes through very strongly, especially on 'Mama Said', while Kirk Hammett's bluesy picking can

a tune about the infamous Kray Brothers, though I personally would have thought it was more likely to be about Ronnie Van Zant. There are a few fillers on 'Load', like the so-so 'Hero Of The Day' and 'Wasting My Hate', but then this really is an experimental album that vastly improves on each subsequent spin.

(LFI)

Metallica being Metallica have always managed to keep up with the times. Only their name tends to pigeon-hole them. The traditional long hair has now given way for a more alternative look, short hair swept back in a greasier style.

The band have also taken to wearing black suits, a look that would look

> ## "Metallica are the only heavy metal band that adults can listen to without feeling their IQ diminishing".
>
> ### Andy Gill, *The Independent*

be heard on the likes of 'Poor Twisted Me' and the ZZ Top influenced 'Ronnie',

(ROSS HALFIN)

more at home in Reservoir Dogs. One other interesting point involves the cover artwork, a dodgy mixture of semen and blood, hence the title 'Load'. Rumour has it that the semen used in the cover artwork was donated by Kirk Hammett. Meanwhile the Metalliwagon rolls on, the band are about to embark on the annual 'Lollapalooza Tour' across the US in June with Soundgarden, Rancid and The Ramones. Metallica will then hit Europe in September.

METALLICA DISCOGRAPHY

UK SINGLES

Jump In The Fire/Seek and Destroy
(live)/Phantom Lord (live)
**Music For Nations PKUT 105
January 1984**

Creeping Death/Am I Evil/Blitzkreig
**Music For Nations 12 KUT 112
November 1984**

The $5.95 EP - Garage Days
Revisited: Helpless/The Small
Hours/The Wait/Crash Course In
Brain Surgery/Last Caress/Green Hell
Vertigo METAL112 August 1987

Harvester Of Sorrow/Breadfan/The
Prince
**Vertigo METAL212
September 1988**

One/For Whom The Bell Tolls (live)/
Welcome Home (Sanitarium) (live)
Vertigo METAL5 April 1989

The Good, The Bad & The Live: The
Six And A Half Year 12" Collection.
Includes all of the above plus The Six
And A Half Year Anniversary Live EP:
Harvester Of Sorrow (live)/One (live)/
Breadfan (live)
Vertigo 8754871 May 1991

Enter Sandman/Stone Cold
Crazy/Holier Than Thou/Enter
Sandman (demo version)
Vertigo METAL7 August 1991

The Unforgiven/Killing Time/So What
**Vertigo METAL8 November
1991**

Nothing Else Matters/Enter Sandman
(live)/Harvester Of Sorrow (live)
Vertigo METAL10 April1992

ALBUMS

KILL 'EM ALL
Hit The Lights/The Four Horsemen/
Motorbreath/Jump In The Fire/
(Anaesthesia) Pulling Teeth/Whiplash/
Phantom Lord/No Remorse/Seek And
Destroy/Metal Militia
**Elektra Entertainment 60766
July 1983**

RIDE THE LIGHTNING
Fight Fire With Fire/Ride The
Lightning/For Whom The Bell
Tolls/Fade To Black/Trapped Under
Ice/Escape/Creeping Death/The Call
Of Ktulu
**Elektra Entertainment 60396
July 1984**

MASTER OF PUPPETS
Battery/Master Of Puppets/The Thing
That Should Not Be/Welcome Home
(Sanitarium)/Disposable Heroes/Leper
Messiah/Orion/Damage Inc
**Elektra Entertainment 60439
February 1986**
(Reissued as a double album, Music
For Nations MFN60DM, January 1987)

...AND JUSTICE FOR ALL
Blackened/...And Justice For All/Eye
Of The Beholder/One/The Shortest
Straw/Harvester Of Sorrow/The Frayed
Ends Of Sanity/To Live Is To Die/Dyers
Eve
**Elektra Entertainment 60812
September 1988**

METALLICA
Enter Sandman/Sad But True/Holier
Than Thou/The Unforgiven/Wherever I
May Roam/Don't Tread On Me/
Through The Never/Nothing Else
Matters/Of Wolf And Man/The God
That Failed/My Friend Of Misery/The
Struggle Within
**Elektra Entertainment 61113
August 1991**

LIVE SHIT: BINGE & PURGE
CD#1: Enter Sandman/Creeping
Death/Harvester of Sorrow/Welcome
Home (Sanitarium)/Sad but True/Of
Wolf & Man/The Unforgiven/Justice
Medley/Solos (Bass/Guitar)
CD#2: Through the Never/For Whom
the Bell Tolls/Fade to Black/Master of
Puppets/Seek & Destroy/Whiplash
CD#3: Nothing Else Matters/
Wherever I May Roam/Am I Evil/Last
Caress/One/Battery/Four Horsemen/
Motorbreath/Stone Cold Crazy
Elektra Entertainment 61594

LOAD
Ain't My Bitch/2X4/The House Jack
Built/Until It Sleeps/King Nothing/
Hero of the Day/Bleeding Me/
Cure/Poor Trusted Me/Wasting My
Hate/Mama Said/Thorn Within/
Ronnie/The Outlaw Tom
**Elektra Entertainment 619223
June 1996**